For stock-car fans who seek mystery and romance.

Phoenix phenomenon.

Vander Ploeg, Fred, & Nelson Miller.

Motor Racing Productions, LLC – May 2024

1527 Pineridge Drive
Grand Haven, MI 49417
USA

ISBN-13: 979-8-89292-855-7

All Rights Reserved
© 2024 Motor Racing Productions, LLC

1

"Championships come with a reckoning," Blake's team owner was saying.

The team owner had gathered his four drivers for a meeting before the Cup championship's final three-race round. The championship race at Phoenix Speedway would follow, after the final round reduced the qualifying drivers from eight to just four.

Four races left in the season. Nine months of racing deciding dozens of races, with just four races left.

"You don't win a championship by stumbling into something," the owner continued, adding, "You don't even win a championship by outworking everyone else, although work certainly helps."

Only two of the team's four drivers remained in the championship hunt. Blake was one of those two drivers, thanks to his dominating Charlotte Roval win in the final race of the prior round.

"What do you mean by a *reckoning*?" one of the drivers asked.

The driver wasn't challenging the team owner's insight. None of the drivers would have. The team owner was not just eminent in stock-car racing and other motorsports. He was also wise. And he wouldn't have minded his drivers desiring to know more of his wisdom, even though he didn't share it often, certainly didn't force it on his drivers or anyone else.

"Something must happen with the driver," the team owner clarified. The team owner tried again, explaining, "Something beyond the driver that the driver recognizes and embraces must enlarge and prepare the driver for the championship."

The four drivers considered the owner's insight. Only Blake among the four drivers looked assured. So the owner continued.

"Championship drivers don't just overcome bigger challenges or more challenges. The championship itself must examine and approve the driver, or the driver won't win the championship."

The drivers all nodded, some because they understood, but others because they didn't want to disappoint the owner. Yet the owner wasn't satisfied with his own articulation. He hadn't yet spoken the truth that called itself out to him. So the owner tried again.

"Drivers win races by resolutely and sensitively applying their considerable skills, with the support of a strong team using the best equipment. But a driver wins a championship only when the championship itself has approved. You don't win a championship. The championship chooses you."

One of the drivers who had not qualified for the final round spoke up, curious.

"If a championship must choose you, how can a driver influence the championship to do so?"

"Now we finally see the issue," the owner replied in satisfaction. He explained, "To win a championship, the driver and team must indeed do everything right. You don't win championships by throwing them away."

The owner paused, searching for the thought. He then continued, "You might win a championship by doing everything right, while hoping the championship comes to you. But championship drivers do more than hope. Championship drivers court championships."

The owner still wasn't satisfied, so he tried again, saying, "Winning a championship isn't a matter of wanting it most. Every driver out there wants it. Some would give their right arm to win just one. But drivers don't grab championships, like they may snatch a race win. Instead, champions *submit* to championships like reluctant kings."

The owner smiled at the thought. He had come closer to describing the challenge of winning a championship than he had thought he might. To lighten the mood, he laughed. The drivers laughed with him.

"Let's just see that one of you figures it out," the owner finally said in the nature of a gentle instruction or princely command. He gave a piercing look at Blake and the other driver who had qualified for the final round.

Blake didn't shy from the team owner's fierce competitiveness. To the contrary, that spirit was what he liked and needed most from his owner. Blake smiled back at the owner, nodding. Challenge accepted. He stole a glance at the other qualifying driver. The driver was looking down, fidgeting with his hands.

Blake later thought deeply about the owner's insight into winning a championship. Blake had seen so many great drivers miss the championship mark. He didn't want to be one of those drivers. Nor did he believe that he would be.

Blake, still young, had just this year confirmed his place among those great drivers. He had won both the Denton 500 and the unprecedented Illianapolis 500 / Sugar-Cola 600 double. Those wins, especially the historic double win, had elevated him to stand among the greats. Yet Blake knew that he must win a Cup championship to cement his pantheon place.

Blake also knew exactly what the team owner had tried to describe. Winning a championship required the championship's cooperation and consent.

Winning a stock-car Cup championship requires passing through a gauntlet. That gauntlet begins with a regular season so long and difficult that it can wear down and break even the finest race teams. Just making the championship playoffs can require many consenting acts of providence.

But then, the playoffs themselves have such a rigorous format. A championship driver must prevail within three brief rounds of three races each. A brief slump in any round, and the driver is out. A championship thus requires a sustained effort precisely when the team's gas tank may have run out.

And then, the championship driver must prevail over the other three qualifying drivers in the championship race itself. Beating other drivers is never a given, even when one has superior equipment and skills. A single blown tire or a single accidental or intentional bump from another driver can ruin a race.

When stock-car racing instituted its playoff system many years ago, traditionalists decried losing the old format where a championship driver could just pile up season-long points, one after another. A champion might never win a race but just consistently finish high enough to prevail on overall points. The old format, while rewarding the enduring slogger, had virtually no fortuity to it.

That predictability is what traditionalists liked. Championship drivers didn't have to court and woo a championship. They didn't have to finesse the championship so that its demons didn't reach up from below to strike at a critical moment with a blown engine or pit-road speeding penalty. The old format eliminated variables and reduced uncertainties, rewarding the one who went to bed early at night.

When many years ago stock-car racing adopted the new playoff format, drivers and teams instantly learned that winning a championship took the championship's consent. The new format had so many variables to it, so many little things that could go wrong, that championship drivers had to both endure and have the favor of providence.

Blake was ready for the challenge. His playoff run, in which he'd had to win the prior race to qualify for the third round, had already suggested that providence might be squarely on his side.

Yet as Blake wrestled with the team owner's challenge late that night, he decided firmly that one never assumes providence's blessing. To do so is to court disaster, not to woo a championship.

The team owner had challenged Blake and the other qualifying driver to get it right, in other words, to discern how to gain a championship's consent. As Blake struggled later into the night to fulfill that challenge, he finally thought he sensed an insight. Perhaps it was the championship-winning insight.

The team owner had suggested that a driver would win the championship not so much on the track against other driver competition but in relation to the championship itself.

What, then, is a championship? A championship stands royally atop a grand hierarchy's pinnacle. A championship is a higher authority, standing over the many lower powers and principalities that make up a grand stock-car season. Indeed, a championship is so high as to be in the divine council itself.

A championship is thus the creator's lieutenant, sent forth in the greatest battles to anoint the chosen one. And a championship anoints only those whom the creator has decided to favor, not on their merit but on the creator's own choice. The driver who won would inherit the creator's choice. The driver who won might not have the greatest skill, equipment, and resources, although skill, equipment, and resources can in themselves be indications of accumulating favor. The driver who won would know that the driver had depended on providence's author.

Somewhere deep in thought as the night wore on, Blake discerned that the only thing the creator lacks is limitation. The creator is all knowing, all good, infinite, eternal, and sovereign, standing over his creation. The creator's only limit is that he is without limit, when limits are in themselves blessings of greater goods.

So, Blake mused, the creator filled that lone void of having no limit by creating limited humans, including flawed stock-car drivers. The creator made creatures with limited life, limited resources, limited wisdom, and limited sight. And, Blake saw, the creator did so in order to have creatures who must depend on him, not because he is arbitrary and capricious but because he is love. The creator, as the ground of being, would elevate his creation.

Thus to woo that author of providence, Blake knew that he must not rely on his own powers and insight alone. He must instead submit to the author, obeying, trusting, and honoring him. But Blake also knew that he could not do so within himself. He must instead give way to the creator's spirit within him so that the spirit could join with the creator. And, Blake also knew, he must do so while discerning and avoiding contrary powers, patterns, and principalities.

Diana longed to see Blake again. After Blake's Charlotte Roval win that propelled him into the final round, Diana and Blake had taken the following day off. Blake took Diana fishing on a nearby lake. Taking Blake's cue to cast her line on the other side, Diana had caught a great fish, on the occasion of which Blake had suggested their wedding date. It would be December 31st.

That was Monday. It was now Wednesday, and both Blake and Diana had hardly had a moment to embrace since. Diana's heart was in Blake's hands, and Blake's heart in hers. But the championship playoffs had both of them in its fiery grip.

Diana didn't begrudge the championship's sway on her fiancé. And good thing for them both. A racer's wife won't do well to regard racing as her husband's mistress. In that case, the mistress might appear to prevail.

Just as Blake had his championship challenge, one that his team owner had pointedly confirmed, so, too, Diana had a challenge. She had a wedding to plan in the midst of supporting Blake in his championship run. And Diana's wedding plan looked very like her own playoffs and championship.

Diana spent Tuesday deep in her own thoughts about how to countenance that challenge. Just as she didn't want to pit her marriage to Blake against Blake's devotion to racing, Diana also didn't want to pit her wedding planning against Blake's championship hunt. The two, wedding planning and championship playoffs, had to come together. If not, the whole thing, marriage and all, might not work.

Diana discerned that she wanted to get her marriage to Blake off on the right foot. Beginnings are important, Diana knew. She remembered her first introduction to Blake, at a splendid luncheon. Fame and friends had surrounded him, and yet Blake had been all kindness, gentleness, humility, and grace. Diana wanted their marriage to have the same aura, the same start, the same foundation.

Diana thus determined to do nothing in wedding preparations that would do anything other than honor and celebrate the concomitant championship chase. In a perfect world, Blake would win the championship because of his impending wedding, not in spite of it, if weddings can have such effects.

And Diana wanted to believe that the union of two into one could indeed exalt both in their individual and joint persons. Diana and Blake had their own careers. Diana had only recently connected her digital journalist's career with stock-car racing, since her courtship with Blake. Yet she could easily see how her marriage to Blake would open more doors for professional opportunity, if that was her calling. But could their marriage also help Blake?

These were the thoughts that occupied Diana when she received a welcome call on Wednesday morning. News that Blake and Diana had set a wedding date just two-and-a-half months away had spread quickly through the driver-and-spouses community. Two wives of stock-car Cup drivers wanted to know if Diana would like some wedding-planning help.

Diana welcomed the offer, not because she would lack the time, skills, or attention. Diana welcomed the offer for the new friends she would make and what she might learn about a good driver marriage.

Diana was joining a rare and special community when marrying a race-car driver. Spouses of doctors, lawyers, pastors, plumbers, or ditch diggers, whatever may be the trade or profession, share things in common. Trades and professions offer their blessings and demand their burdens not just for the one carrying out the work but also for the spouse of the wage earner. The spouse of an ER doctor or obstetrician knows that the work has no time bounds.

Wives of race-car drivers learn more than how to accommodate their husband's crazy schedule. They learn more than how to help their husband make peace with danger, risk, and loss. They learn more than patience and endurance. They also learn how to cultivate racing's field to bless the marriage.

No one should feel sorry for the spouse of a race-car driver, especially a driver so skilled and successful as to compete in the stock-car Cup series. A driver's wife has special challenges but also special opportunities, not just for travel, fame, and fortune, but also to make a special marriage. Diana wanted to learn what she could.

That the driver's wives were from other race teams didn't entirely surprise Diana. She had already seen how willing wives were to support one another across teams and even across racing series. Diana had made good acquaintances among the race wives, although she couldn't say yet that she had made good friends. Diana wanted lasting friendships among the race wives.

The two wives offered to meet Diana over lunch in downtown Charlotte that Wednesday. Time was of the essence, they all agreed. All three would shortly be traveling to Las Vegas for the next race that weekend. Diana slipped away from work to meet them.

"What's your biggest fear?" one wife asked after they had settled at a table and exchanged some pleasantries.

"That Blake doesn't show up," the other wife joked, at which they all laughed.

"I don't know that I have any fears," Diana said, considering the question, "Other than maybe my dress being too tight."

Again, they all laughed.

"No, really," the first wife said again, "What is it you don't want to happen? If you know the one regret you could have, maybe we can help you avoid it."

"Yes," Diana agreed, while admitting, "I just don't want to feel afterward like the whole wedding plan was bigger than Blake and I, bigger in a sense than our marriage."

"So maybe you'd prefer something simpler," the second wife asked.

"Definitely," Diana answered, "Except that something too simple wouldn't be honoring Blake and our marriage in the way that it deserves."

"I felt the same way, Honey," the first wife agreed as she reached across the small table and put her hand on Diana's arm.

The second wife nodded in agreement, saying, "So something grand but simple."

"Yes," Diana said, "Very grand, but maybe grand because of its simplicity."

The two wives nodded, one joking, "So we're all headed to Vegas for this next playoff race, but that's not the place for wedding inspiration?"

The three of them laughed again.

"And I'd guess not Talladega, Texas, or Atlanta, either?" the other wife asked with a big smile.

"No, not Vegas or any of those other big speedways as wedding inspiration," Diana confirmed with another chuckle.

"So if you wanted your wedding to be like *some* racetrack, not *at* the track but *like* the track, which track would it be?" one of the wives asked.

The two wives waited with big smiles, enjoying the humor. Diana thought for another moment, her mind running through the racetracks.

"Not Sonoma. Not a wine-country wedding, although that doesn't sound so bad," Diana began. She continued, "And not Pocono. Not a green country wedding. And not Chicago. Not a big urban bash."

Diana looked into the distance, her eyes beginning to fill with joyful tears.

"You want a Charlotte wedding, Honey," one of the wives said, "Direct, honest, decent, grand, and simple."

Diana nodded. Then, she laughed, saying, "Just not the Roval." The other two wives laughed with her.

2

"Tell me more of this *phenomenon* you're sensing, Big Guy," Rob urged Blake, adding, "It sounds like you're onto something."

Blake had spent Tuesday and Wednesday strategizing with his race team while getting lap after lap on the simulator under the watchful eye of the race engineer and data analyst. The team's race haulers left for Las Vegas early on Wednesday. By the time Blake and the other drivers flew out, the haulers would be there already.

Las Vegas Motor Speedway was a familiar and friendly track for Blake. He'd run well there before, although he had yet to win. The track treated the team's other three drivers well, too, especially the other driver to qualify for the final round. That driver had won the Vegas race earlier in the year.

For Blake, the simulator work was a tune up, a reminder to get the muscle memory working again. He didn't expect a revelation from the simulator work, and he got none.

Blake's mind was instead on what he had begun to call his *phenomenon* issue, one that the team owner's challenge had raised. Blake had mentioned the team owner's challenge to his friend and brother-in-law Rob, the husband of Blake's sister Marla. Marla handled public relations for Blake.

As a military PSYOPS veteran, Rob was attuned to phenomena. Rob knew the power of the mind to discern patterns and even powers and principles that the eye could not see or the hands touch. Rob also knew the power of deception, when patterns and principles distorted the mind's perception.

Blake had taken a break from race preparation on Tuesday evening, long enough to stop by Rob's residence. Rob helped stock-car racing, Blake's team, and Blake with security. Blake thus made it a practice to stay in close touch with Rob. But Rob also had a wise and discerning mind. Rob saw significant things others did not.

Marla met Blake at the door, giving him a sister's hug and kiss on the cheek. They hadn't seen one another since Blake and Diana had set the wedding date.

"December 31st, huh?" Marla smiled up at Blake.

Blake nodded with a wide smile.

"She's excited, isn't she?" Marla asked.

Blake nodded again, still smiling.

Marla had already stopped by to see Diana at work, dropping off a little gift and leaving a word of encouragement. Marla was ready to help Diana. They'd already made plans about a wedding dress.

"He's out back on the patio waiting for you," Marla said to Blake.

Blake and Rob had a good discussion. Blake admitted that until the team owner had issued his challenge, Blake had always thought of pursuing the championship. He hadn't thought of the championship choosing him.

"Oh, yes," Rob had agreed with the point, "It's a well-recognized cognitive or philosophical construct that phenomena speak their meaning and purpose. We recognize things, even things so simple as a cup or chair, only because they call to us with their purpose."

Blake nodded, waiting for Rob to continue.

"A championship could do the same thing," Rob said after a pause to collect his thoughts. "A championship can both have influence and accept influence, phenomenologically. The primary debate is whether phenomena have agency, choosing their course, or not."

Blake nodded, saying with a smile, "Spooky stuff."

Rob laughed, nodding while replying, "Yes, the ancients certainly would have referred to gods and demons. Moderns prefer to talk about aggregate beings, egregores, non-physical entities, or collective thoughts."

Once again, Blake nodded, hoping Rob would continue. Rob tracked with Blake's thoughts often, unusual for a brother in law. Soon enough, Rob did continue.

"A phenomenon isn't quite the same as an apparition or phantom," Rob tried, "But one could say that once one conceives an apparition or phantom, it is as consequential as a phenomenon. One must deal with both the real and the perceived, sometimes with equal commitment."

"What do you think the championship signifies?" Blake asked, already having a good sense of his own answer.

"Oh, not much doubt about that, is there, Big Guy?" Rob replied with a laugh, adding, "But I get what you mean. As a phenomenon, the championship is a higher-order entity, one with special powers. We see those powers at work all around us, especially in this crazy playoff time."

Blake smiled, saying, "We're quite familiar with those powers, aren't we?"

"Yes," Rob agreed, "Both positive and negative in their influence and effect."

Blake had another question, though.

"How about Phoenix?" Blake asked, "What does it signify?"

Blake was referring to Phoenix Speedway, where in the season's last race the champion must finish ahead of the other three qualifying drivers.

"Now that's an interesting phenomenon," Rob replied, adding, "A phoenix in classical mythology is of course the desert bird that burns itself on a funeral pyre, only to rise renewed out of the ashes."

Rob was silent for a moment, considering.

"I suppose I hadn't thought of it before," Rob finally admitted, "But the phoenix phenomenon has its own influence, both inside and outside of classical mythology, and for that matter inside and outside stock-car racing."

"What do you mean?" Blake asked, although again, he had already surmised his own answer.

"Well," Rob replied, "The phoenix gains a sort of immortality, but only a wearying one that requires a perpetual cycle of death and rebirth."

"Like circling a racetrack without victory, without end," Blake observed wryly.

"Indeed, when a championship driver needs to instead rise above the racetrack in immortality," Rob replied.

"Classicists, and Egyptians and Persians, too, associated the phoenix with the sun," Rob continued, "Giving the myth the echoes of Prometheus stealing fire from the gods. Prometheus gave humankind technology, greater power over its own ends. Of course, Zeus punished Prometheus with eternal agony, not too different from the phoenix dying on a funeral pyre over and over again."

Blake and Rob fell silent as they watched the night steal the sun from the patio.

"What's the practical application?" Blake finally asked.

Again, Blake only wanted Rob's confirmation of a kernel of an idea Blake already held. And Rob didn't hesitate.

"You and I both know the answer," Rob said with a sly smile, adding, "The desert is a place where technology fails, a place of pyrrhic victories, victories that consume like the phoenix. Respect the higher-order powers of the championship but remember that the championship is not the highest power. For true victory, one must follow the ways of the author of all things, including the championship. Pay too much attention to the phenomenon of the championship, and you'll lose sight of how its author controls and directs it."

Just as Rob finished, Blake's watch buzzed with a text message. Blake looked down at it.

"Hmm," he reacted, "Something's up. I'd better run."

Rob raised his eyebrows. Pointing to Blake's watch, Rob said, "Sounds like the championship's already got a hold of someone."

Blake looked back, surprised at Rob's inference, saying only, "Maybe so. Maybe so."

Blake was back at the team's facility in minutes. He went straight to his crew chief's office. The crew chief and race engineer looked up as Blake entered.

"I don't know what's gotten into him," the crew chief began, "It's like the final round's pressure is too much or something."

"Did something happen between the two of you?" the race engineer asked.

Blake shook his head. He and the team's other driver still in the championship hunt were friends and fellow supporters. But Blake thought back to the team owner's challenge. Blake hadn't liked the way the other driver had responded. Maybe it was the pressure.

"Tell me what happened," Blake asked calmly, trying already to relieve the concern.

"First was the simulator argument," the race engineer replied in an irritated manner, adding, "He didn't feel like he had equal time, so he went ahead and changed our schedule."

Blake shrugged, saying, "We'll be alright. I'm ahead with the simulator work, and we've still got time tomorrow, right?"

The race engineer nodded once but interjected, "It's not just who gets to use it. It's what they've done with it."

"What do you mean?" Blake asked with a greater note of concern.

"I haven't been able to run any simulations since they last used it," the race engineer replied, adding, "So they said to use their data. But their data doesn't look right to me."

Blake didn't know how to answer. Simulations were key to testing dozens of possible car setups. If they couldn't use the simulator, they might be at a distinct disadvantage.

"It works fine for them but won't work at all for me," the race engineer concluded.

Blake looked to his crew chief.

"I've already got a call out to the simulator manufacturer," the crew chief said, adding, "I'm sure they'll help us figure it out first thing tomorrow in time for some more simulator work."

"How can I help?" Blake asked both of them.

"Can you talk with him?" the race engineer asked, adding, "I've not seen him act like that before. It didn't even seem like him."

Blake nodded, saying, "We'll chat tomorrow. Anything left that we can do tonight?"

"I'll keep running their numbers," the race engineer replied, "But I don't want to use their data unless I'm sure it's right. We might be winging it this weekend."

"Let's hope not," the crew chief said sternly.

Blake headed home thinking of one thing: *team dynamics*.

Stock-car racing, Blake knew, has a lore of team dynamics. One-driver teams don't have driver dynamics. The dynamics are all within the one-car team. Driver can still disagree with the crew chief who may disagree with the race engineer. And the owner may disagree with them all. But they'll work things out according to the hierarchies that order them.

Two, three, and four-car teams are different. Multi-car teams have the advantage of learning from one another. The success or failure of the setups on one car can inform the setup on another car, and vice versa.

But multi-car teams can also compete for resources, personnel, simulator time, and dozens of other priorities. The success of one car could draw attention and resources away from another car to the detriment of one or both.

Multi-car teams thus require constant balancing. They can also require an owner to step in and set things right, although owners would generally far prefer that drivers and crew chiefs work things out themselves.

Blake would have preferred to be thinking about the coming Las Vegas race. But he was willing to have a chat with the other qualifying driver. Maybe he could work something out. Something told him, though, that he needed wiser counsel. Blake was already feeling like the championship was leading him down a path he ought not go.

As soon as Blake got home, he pulled his cellphone from his pocket and gave it a few taps.

"Yes, Fred, Blake here," Blake said into the cellphone when the one on the other end had answered. "We may have a team dynamic. Do you have a few minutes to give me your thoughts?"

Blake knew he could trust Fred, who was a tech official in his stock-car life but a psychologist outside of it, for both wisdom and confidentiality. Blake spent the next couple of minutes filling Fred in.

"Yes," Fred replied, "It could be a manifestation of playoff pressure. But you've not heard his side of the story yet, so better not jump to any conclusions. If it's playoff pressure, then you know how to defuse small conflicts while taking big conflicts to the boss. Just know that your race engineer may be reflecting pressure, too. I know you'll give him your support, too. Welcome to the championship race, huh?"

Blake chuckled at Fred's humor.

"Oh, and one more thought," Fred added, "Your adversary isn't your team's other playoff driver. Don't make an adversary of a person, position, or event. Your adversary is beyond sight, influencing those persons and things that oppose you. My guess is that you're coming face to face with the Phoenix phenomenon. Your adversary in this championship has appeared in deceptive guise, which is the way the adversary works."

Fred stopped, letting Blake digest his thoughts. Then he shared one last thought.

"Bring coffee and donuts tomorrow morning," Fred laughed, adding, "That'll probably do the trick, right?"

Blake joined in Fred's laughter.

That night, Blake dreamed of phantoms, demons, and apparitions. None of his dreams made any sense. They were just random nightmares. Ghostlike entities moved in and out, leaving their fears and frustrations. The dreams had no context to them. Blake wasn't racing, fishing, or eating out. He was just encountering frightening apparitions without clear material entities. He was in a fallen realm in which the powers could only frighten, not consume. The last one of those nightmares woke Blake early.

Rather than fall asleep again, only to endure more apparitions, Blake decided to get up and head straight to the bakery for donuts. He then stopped by the coffee shop on his way to the team facility. Well equipped, he headed straight for the other qualifying driver's office. Blake found him in his office, feet up on the desk, watching YouTube videos. He smiled as Blake walked in with the coffee and donuts.

"For me?" the driver smiled broadly at Blake, adding in jest, "You shouldn't have! What have you done wrong that you owe me?!"

Blake laughed at the driver's jest.

"Everything alright between us?" Blake asked.

"Of course," the driver said, "Why?"

Blake hadn't expected such a jovial welcome. So he tried again.

"Any issue with simulator time or anything else?"

"Of course not, Buddy," the driver replied, "We've never given one another problems with something so small as that. You're a simulator ace, anyway."

"How's the simulator data working for you?" Blake tried one more time, adding, "Heading in the right direction?"

"Seems so," the driver replied, adding, "The engineer and analyst are satisfied, anyway. All seems to be in order. Off to Vegas, huh?"

Blake was nonplussed. He decided not to try again. *Why plant weeds where none grow?* he thought.

"Hey, hold on," Blake joked as the driver tried to take the whole box of donuts, "They're not *all* for you. I've got other friends to make, too."

They laughed. Blake held the box open. The driver grabbed two donuts.

"Keep your coffee, friend," the driver said as he lifted a mug, "I've got my own special brew. And say hello to that wonderful woman of yours. So, December 31st is the date?"

Blake nodded, winked, and headed out.

As he headed for his own office, Blake wondered whether he had just encountered his first championship phantom. The simulator issue certainly seemed like an apparition.

3

"Alright, so time to get down to business," Marla said with a smile at Diana. As they settled into the diner's booth, Marla added, "What are your thoughts on the dress?"

Diana, Marla, and Rob had flown out to Las Vegas late on Thursday. Blake was already there, having flown out with the other drivers early that day.

Having little to do Friday morning, Diana and Marla had scheduled some wedding-planning time. The track hadn't offered a private place, so they had slipped away to a nearby diner.

Desert sun streamed through the diner's tinted window. The temperature outside was already rising.

"It's a big deal, the dress, isn't it?" Diana replied with a smile.

"You're the show's star, Honey," Marla replied with a laugh, adding, "And a fitting star you are."

Diana looked down with a shy smile while replying, "Maybe that's my challenge with the dress. I don't feel like I want to be the star or that the wedding should be a show."

"Then that tells us what we need to know about the dress," Marla agreed. Marla thought for a moment before adding, "Yet your wedding is a celebration not just for you and Blake but also for the stock-car racing family. It's one of the greater things we do."

Diana nodded. The two sat in silence for a few moments.

"Hey," Marla soon said, "I've got an idea. Let's go look at some dresses."

"Right now?" Diana asked.

"Sure, why not?" Marla replied.

"But two drivers' wives have already offered their help," Diana objected.

"Give them a call," Marla suggested, adding, "Maybe they'll join us. I'm sure they're here."

"That would be fun," Diana agreed.

Half an hour later, the four women were in a wedding shop on the Vegas strip.

"Does this look bad?" Diana asked as the four of them met at the shop, "I mean, like in a few minutes we're heading to the little chapel down the street?"

The other women laughed, one saying, "Hey, Baby, if that's what it takes."

They all laughed again.

The next half hour was more of the same. The four women teased, joked, and laughed together at all that women go through in a courtship, engagement, wedding, and marriage. It was exactly what Diana needed, both a rite of passage and a welcome into married life.

They also found the dress. It was elegant in its simplicity, alluring in its spare adornment, and pure in its form.

As Diana thought of it later, she realized how much is indeed in the dress, how much in a wedding, how much in a marriage. The dress manifests all for which husbands and wives, the divorced and the widowed, singles and engaged, young and old, and even children all yearn. The dress is poise, purity, enchantment, allure, inspiration, aspiration, and eternity.

The dress draws together time and space, both calling the future into being while declaring the bold and hopeful present, past, present, and future all captured in the single form of the dress, broad at the base like the creator's mountain, gathered upward into the heart where resides the spirit's breath. Diana was both relieved and glad that they had found the dress.

"Does Blake need to approve?" Diana asked, as she spun around again in front of the mirror and her friends, modeling the dress.

"Oh, Baby," one wife replied with a kind smile, "Only you would know."

"Are you going to start him off that way?" the other wife teased, "You better just go for it."

They all laughed again. And on the fun went.

Blake and the race team were hard at work in the garage back at the racetrack, getting ready for practice. One of the mechanics, though, was having fits, frustrated over recalcitrant parts.

"That's the third time I've replaced it," the mechanic was saying to the crew chief, "And it still doesn't seem right."

"Do you have another one handy?" the crew chief asked, adding, "Sometimes the new ones have a defect, too."

"No," the mechanic replied, "I just swapped in the last one."

"How about back in the hauler?" the crew chief asked.

"I don't think so, but I'll check," the mechanic said in a desultory manner.

"Hey, look," the crew chief scolded, "It's alright. If the hauler doesn't have another one, just walk over and borrow one from one of our other crews."

The mechanic gave the crew chief a stern look, saying, "I already did. They refused."

The crew chief raised his eyebrows.

"Who refused?" the crew chief said indignantly.

The mechanic jerked his head in the direction of the next garage stall, where another one of the team's crews was working on the other qualifying driver's car.

"I'll be right back," the crew chief said with a note of anger.

"Hey, what's up?" Blake called to the crew chief from the back of the garage where Blake was leaning on a tool cabinet.

Blake had watched the whole exchange between the mechanic and crew chief. That was Blake's habit, to spend as much time as he could in the garage when anyone was working on or around his car. If Blake didn't have ideas for what he wanted done with his car, he at least wanted to know what ideas others had. Blake wanted to know everything about his race car.

Hearing Blake's voice, the crew chief stopped. He looked over toward Blake with a scowl. Blake smiled and gave a tip of his head, inviting the crew chief over. The crew chief hesitated, thinking that he might just go tell the other crew a thing or two. But thinking better of it, the crew chief joined Blake at the back of the garage.

"The nerve of them," the crew chief told Blake, "Like they're not going to need a part from *us* some day."

"Look," Blake smiled at the crew chief again, "It's not worth the frustration. It's probably a misunderstanding. Give it a little while. Bring it up with their crew chief later, alone, after practice, if you still feel you need to do so."

"What about the part?" the crew chief asked, adding, "I'm not letting you out on that track until it's replaced and working right."

"Didn't you say we might have another in the hauler?" Blake asked.

The crew chief nodded.

"And don't we have two other crews on our team we could ask?" Blake asked again, with another easy smile.

The crew chief nodded again. He shrugged, said *I'll be right back* to the mechanic, and headed for the hauler.

Blake breathed a sigh of relief, chalking the episode up to another apparition. More Phoenix phenomenon, Blake thought again.

Practice was otherwise uneventful. Despite the simulator issues, Blake's race engineer had arrived at a satisfactory setup. Blake, the race engineer, and the crew chief made a few tweaks, but the car had unloaded in good shape and performed well from the start.

That night, away from the garage and alone with his thoughts, Blake reflected back over the day's challenges, more than the day's successes.

Blake wasn't worried about the team, despite cracks in its facade of confidence. Blake interpreted those cracks not so much as human eccentricities and failures. He trusted his team, including their ability to withstand championship stresses while continuing to do their jobs with aplomb.

Blake instead saw those fissures in the wall as evidence of another realm's operation. Blake had come to accept that higher-order constructs, whether playoffs or championships or even the concept of pressure, had their agency. They had their gods or demons, as it were. Blake wasn't at all surprised that their agency would manifest itself in disagreements, conflicts, confusion, and frustration.

Yet Blake also discerned that the way to counteract the action, influence, and agency of playoff and championship demons was to appeal to even higher-order constructs. One thwarted the demon *pressure* with the wisdom *perspective*. One subsumed the deity *playoffs* with the construct *eternity*. One trumped the avatar *championship* with the creator's greater *triumph*.

Blake didn't attempt to force poise and equanimity on turbulent circumstances. He instead met the turbulence head on with its conquering order.

Blake knew that one does not cover chaotic waters, stirred into storm by such things as championship aspirations. One cannot use ordinary means to counteract extraordinary forces. To do so is to risk drowning in those waters. One instead draws the golden fish from those chaotic waters.

Blake saw that the final three playoff races and championship race were going to unleash more hellhounds around the garage, race shop, and race track. Adventure confronts demons as it scales the mountain seeking the holy grail. Blake didn't begrudge the demons their demonic work.

Who knows, Blake even thought, but that the fiends might come after him and Diana as they planned and relished their wedding? But Blake fell sound asleep assured that both he and Diana knew that they need only to look to their greater creator.

That night, both Blake and Diana dreamed the same dream, although each in their own context.

Blake's dream was of phantasmagoric entities besetting his race preparation, one after another. No sooner had Blake and his team more or less avoided one catastrophe than the demons were coordinating another. Blake couldn't even get his car on the track. And the entities weren't just spoiling races. They were getting ever nearer consuming Blake.

Diana's dream was of similar entities besetting her wedding preparations. No sooner would Diana and her friends more or less avert one disaster than the demons would hatch another. Diana couldn't even make it to the wedding, and Blake was nowhere in sight. The demons were encircling Diana, intent on taking her life.

When Blake and Diana met briefly the next morning, they looked in one another's eyes. In doing so, they sensed the struggle that the other had endured through the long, dream-soaked night. But they also sensed that the struggle had been victorious. No dream was going to shake their faith in their creator or in one another. Indeed, in the dreams, they saw only their creator's call to his higher path.

Blake and Diana had such confidence in their creator and in one another because they understood, intuitively if not expressly, that they each existed only as they remained connected with their creator. They each knew, intuitively if not expressly, that only their creator is self-existent, carrying being within him to share with the creatures whom he creates.

Blake and Diana trusted in their creator because they saw that their reason and purpose, and indeed their very being, depended on him alone. They had no existence other than in their place as his beloved children. And no demon could deny them that inheritance.

Blake took to the racetrack later that day to qualify for the next day's playoff race. Blake liked Las Vegas Motor Speedway for its traditional mile-and-a-half oval and its steep progressive banking, up to twenty degrees at the top. Blake thought of himself first as an oval racer, as many stock-car racers do. He also liked the side-by-side racing of a speedway with progressive banking, for its aerodynamics and other technical and tactical challenges.

Qualifying went pretty much as Blake and his crew chief had hoped. They had spent hours discussing strategy for the first of the three playoff races in this final round. By the end of the final round, after all three races, Blake had to be behind no more than three of the playoff drivers, to make the championship race. That meant that Blake had to beat at least four of the playoff drivers.

The final playoff round wasn't, in other words, simply a matter of playing it safe so as to avoid finishing near the bottom. It wasn't like the first round, in which twelve of sixteen drivers advanced, nor even like the second round in which eight of twelve drivers advanced. In this final round, Blake had to finish in the top half of the eight playoff drivers, or his championship effort would be over.

Blake, his crew chief, and the race engineer thus dialed up the risk, to reach for the reward. Both for qualifying and for the race, Blake would drive closer to the edge than he had early in the prior rounds. He would enter the turns with slightly greater speed, ride lower on the curves, and come closer to the wall on exit, trusting that his setup would hold the grip.

Diana was atop Blake's pit box for qualifying. She watched as car after car from the field completed their qualifying lap. The times improved as the drivers' places in the points standings improved, until the eight playoff drivers began their qualifying runs, one by one.

The first playoff driver bested the rest of the field, knocking a tenth of a second off the prior best qualifying time. The second playoff driver beat the first playoff driver by a couple hundredths of a second more.

Diana listened over her radio headset to Blake's crew chief giving Blake final instructions for his qualifying lap, as the third playoff driver began his qualifying run. Diana watched that driver's car dive too low into the first turn. The car wiggled and then quickly crept its way up the great bank until it tapped the outer wall.

The driver saved the car from an outright crash. But the tap on the wall and the driver's lifting the accelerator ruined the qualifying run. The driver finished with a qualifying time near the bottom. The driver's crew would work on the car all night, and the driver would start at the back of the pack.

Blake's car was already up to speed on its warmup lap. Diana heard Blake's crew chief briefly tell Blake of the prior car's wiggle and slide. Diana took a deep breath, wondering whether Blake would take the same risk as the driver ahead of him and suffer the same fate.

Blake's car flashed across the starting line and toward the first curve. Starting on the track's outside, Blake expertly turned his car down low to the track's inside entering the turn, but not as low as the prior car had tried. Blake also held a higher line around the curve. After blazing down the backstretch, Blake took the same approach to the next great banked curve, not as low and not as tight. Out of the second curve Blake's car flew.

At the finish line, Blake had bested the field but not either of the first two playoff drivers. He had played it a little more conservatively than he might have done, if his intent had been to take the pole. Learning from Blake's line, the last few playoff cars to follow him also bested Blake's time. Blake would start in seventh, behind all the other playoff drivers except the one who had nearly crashed.

Diana climbed down from atop the pit box to walk back to the garage, just as Blake navigated his car off pit road and along the same garage lane. Diana peered into Blake's car as it rolled right by her side. Seeing Diana's searching look inside his car, Blake gave her a thumbs up. Diana beamed. The final round was underway, with Blake satisfied. Diana breathed a sigh of relief.

4

"Come on, Big Guy," Rob urged Blake, "I've got someone for you to meet."

Qualifying was over. Blake had spent hours poring over the results with his crew chief and the race engineer.

Blake qualifying seventh wasn't a problem. Sunday's race at Las Vegas Motor Speedway was the South Point 400. The racers and their teams would have hundreds of miles and several pit stops, under green and cautions, to fine tune their cars for the last stage and critical final run.

The teams had also used qualifying trim, meaning setups emphasizing short-run speed, for their qualifying runs. They would revert to race trim for the start of the race. That might mean tire pressure changes, coil and shock adjustments, and other small or large adjustments for longer-run speed. Qualifying results might not mean all that much for how the cars would perform during the race with their different setups.

But Blake, his crew chief, and the race engineer still spent hours considering what they might learn about racing lines, track compound, and car setup from the qualifying results. They also worked into Saturday evening confirming their race strategy for the next day's event.

Rob waited for Blake at the garage until Blake was done. They routinely spend some down time together late on the night before a race, not for further analysis but to relax and maybe to lightly process any remaining open ends.

This evening, though, Rob had an introduction to make. He guided Blake toward a short, bearded man perched comfortably on a hiker's folding chair, more like a simple sling.

The man had evidently been waiting for Rob to make the introduction because he hopped up, snapping his small sling shut into a hiking stick, as Rob and Blake approached.

Blake had never seen anyone quite like this small, somewhat heavyset, bearded man, anywhere near a racetrack. His long, full beard and peculiar outdoor clothing, not to mention his hiking sling and a rough leather knapsack thrown over one shoulder, made him look more like a gnome or troll than a race fan.

Blake would later learn from Rob that the man indeed lived off the grid in a yurt in the mountains near Phoenix Speedway. The man had the perfect dress and appearance for that peculiar lifestyle, not for a stock-car race within a short drive of the Las Vegas strip.

Yet as out of place as the peculiar man looked, Blake somehow took an instant liking to him. Perhaps it was the glint in the man's eyes or maybe his self-deprecating demeanor or the deeply thoughtful, hesitant, and precise way in which the man spoke. But whatever attracted Blake to the man, Blake had an instant sense that Rob had somehow made yet another valuable connection.

As it turned out, Rob had long known the yurt man, from exactly what encounter neither could quite recall. They had somehow just discovered that they shared an interest in the same things. Call it philosophy, theology, epistemology, spirituality, symbolism, narrative, or whatever you will.

For as long as Rob had been traveling with stock-car racing to Phoenix Speedway, Rob had made a point to visit the nearby yurt man. Those visits had always left Rob informed, perhaps even enchanted or spellbound.

Rob and the yurt man had even begun to stay in touch in between Phoenix races, after Rob had helped the yurt man acquire solar panels and batteries for enough power for a satellite internet connection. The yurt man wasn't anti-technology, at least when technology might expand his intellectual horizons.

After a brief introduction, the yurt man first apologized to Blake for interrupting his evening.

Blake blinked, wordless. Blake found himself politely saying *no need to apologize*, even though Blake had no idea of the man's intentions.

To move their conversation quickly along to its point and relieve the man of the awkwardness of their late-evening encounter, Rob suggested that they head to Rob's car. Blake looked blankly at Rob, still unsure of the purpose of the encounter. Taking Blake's hint, Rob explained.

"We need to return my friend to the bus terminal," Rob said to Blake as the three of them turned and walked slowly toward Rob's car in the distant parking lot.

"He's come from outside Phoenix by bus to share a message, insight, or proposal with you," Rob continued, although here he paused to look at his peculiar friend, who shrugged as if to say *yes, that's the nature of it*.

"He needs to catch his bus back tonight," Rob continued, adding, "I think we'll just make it. You were rather later than either of us expected."

Rob smiled at Blake, who nodded politely while saying, "Yes, we were quite late, and I'm sorry about that," although Blake remained astonished at the thought of the man's inconvenient travel and peculiar purpose.

"So, if we can get to the point," the man said to Blake.

Blake once again nodded, although still entirely baffled and bemused at the peculiar man. All Blake could think was that Rob had really pulled one out of his hat this time. Blake assumed that they'd have a good laugh about it later.

Yet for the next twenty minutes as they walked to Rob's car and then headed to the bus terminal, the man spoke of profound insights Blake had never heard before, mixed with other insights Blake had barely discerned but had lacked the language to articulate. The man's quiet explanations of phenomena familiar to Blake stunned Blake for the depth, order, and freshness of their insights, even though the explanations seemed entirely trustworthy and even conventional once so simply and elegantly expressed.

For as long as their brief conversation lasted, Blake felt as if he was seeing new dimensions of truth that should have been obvious to him, had he only considered. The man wasn't a mystic. He wasn't sharing hidden special knowledge. He was instead just speaking of things that years of living alone in a yurt, with the sole purpose of considering the nature of the universe and its creator, had finally taught him. And he was speaking of them with a hesitant humility that entirely endeared Blake to him.

They had reached the bus terminal. The yurt man had to be quickly off if he was going to just catch his bus back to Phoenix.

All that Blake could say as they parted was *let's stay in touch*, not out of politeness but because Blake meant it. Blake watched the yurt man shuffle quickly off, as Rob circled his car out of the bus terminal.

"I thought you'd appreciate meeting my friend," Rob said quietly to Blake as they motored off into the night, adding, "Especially with the anomalies you'll be facing in this championship pursuit."

Blake looked at Rob who stole a glance back as he headed the car back to the racetrack. Rob had a great smile on his face, just like one who had seen his two favorite friends meet for the first time.

Blake shook his head as if to clear it of the man's powerful spell. As he did so, Blake chuckled in quiet appreciation for the unpredictably profound quality of the encounter, as if he simply could not believe it.

"Am I dreaming?" Blake asked.

"Maybe," Rob replied. And they both laughed.

"That was certainly insightful," Blake remarked, "But he didn't exactly say what his proposal was."

Rob gave Blake another sidelong glance as he made his way along the Vegas strip back toward the track.

"He's too shy to say it," Rob replied.

"Say what?"

"He wants to help you win the championship."

Blake guffawed in disbelief. But even as he did so, he regretted it.

"I'm sorry," Blake said, "I'm still just a bit staggered."

"That's alright, Pardner," Rob said with a smile, "He can have that effect on others. He definitely comes from another time and place. And he wouldn't have liked me saying he wanted to help you win. He would instead have called it an *experiment*, a *test of his hypothesis*."

Blake thought about the yurt man's proposition the rest of their way back to the track.

As Rob pulled up in the parking lot to drop off Blake, Blake turned to Rob, saying with a serious look, "I'm in."

"I knew you would be," Rob replied with a warm smile, adding, "We're in it together, then."

Rob reached over and shook Blake's hand with a firm, celebratory grip.

Race day dawned as six out of seven Las Vegas mornings dawn. The sun leapt into the sky and beamed across the track. The track's crew welcomed the sun's warmth in the cool morning.

Diana met Marla at the track's parking lot for a morning walk. Marla would soon be busy with her public-relations work. Diana readily consented to follow Marla checking out the track's race control loge boxes where Marla would be making her corporate sponsor contacts for Blake before and during the race.

The track looked spectacular in the still, cool, sunny morning, as they stepped from the enclosed loge out into the open boxes well above the track. Diana and Marla stopped side by side, taking the gorgeous view in. A vast crowd would soon throng the place. But for the moment, the place and moment were pristine.

"What are you thinking, Gal?" Marla asked as she watched Diana stare serenely across the track and into the distance.

"Wouldn't be a bad place for a wedding," Diana remarked casually with a smile.

"Vegas?" Marla replied with more than a hint of doubt.

"Well, not necessarily here," Diana said, "But at a beautiful racetrack. I've been thinking about it since we joked about it the other day. It might not be a bad idea at all."

"The Speedway Club at Charlotte," Marla replied, "That's what you're thinking."

"Yes," Diana replied, again looking into the distance.

"Blake would be fine with that, wouldn't he?" Marla asked.

Diana laughed, saying, "Yes, he would. It just seems fitting."

Marla and Diana didn't need to say it to one another, but they were both thinking of Blake's spectacular win of Charlotte Motor Speedway's Sugar-Cola 600 earlier that year, capping his unprecedented open-wheel / stock-car double.

"Want me to broach it with him?" Marla offered, adding, "He and I have some corporate contacts to make later this morning."

Diana turned to Marla with a smile, saying, "That would be nice."

"We may have to pull some strings to get it," Marla cautioned.

"Oh, I know," Diana replied, adding, "Let's hope not too hard or too many."

They both laughed.

A moment passed before Marla said, "Wow, two big things off your wedding list, the dress and the venue. Vegas has been good to you."

"We'll soon see just how good," Diana replied, motioning toward the racetrack below.

Race day moved with its usual methodical rhythm, one to which Diana had grown accustomed across the long season. Driver introductions finally came and soon passed. Diana stood with Blake for the anthem, ready to take her place atop the pit box, alone with her thoughts. And Blake was in the car and off.

Some of the season's races had captured and engrossed Diana, as if she was riding in the car with Blake. Diana experienced the ups and downs of those races emotionally, viscerally. She would stand and shout in excitement, sit with her fists clenched to her mouth in fear, and breathe huge sighs of relief, while Blake's car madly circled the track.

Other races, though, entranced Diana, moving her emotions to a far-off place where she seemed to watch the race from an ancient past or distant future. She saw those races as if through a telescope, rather than through the usual microscope of emotions. And other races affected her in other ways.

Diana hadn't yet discerned why races had their kaleidoscopic effects. Maybe she hadn't experienced enough races yet, still in her first stock-car season, to know where a race might land on the rich spectrum of experiences and reactions.

As Diana settled in atop Blake's pit box for the race, she looked deep inside herself for hints of its emerging effect. She also resolved to ask her new driver's wife friends about their own experiences.

This race, though, turned out not to be Diana's to experience. Throughout the race, Diana had little impression of her own response. She had neither the exciting, visceral reactions to the race's ups and downs nor the distant, timeless perspective of the race unfolding layers of her own life.

Instead, Diana experienced the race as Blake experienced it. From the moment Diana donned the radio headset, handed back to her by the race engineer sitting in front of her atop the pit box, the race engrossed her with Blake's own thoughts.

Diana could tell that Blake struggled throughout the race to manage his balky and fitful car, apply his crew chief's suggested strategies, and instantly process his spotter's observations. Diana heard those struggles in Blake's voice. The crew chief, race engineer, and spotter sounded as clear, confident, and decisive as ever. Blake, though, did not. He seemed to be fighting something beyond the racetrack, car, and racing conditions.

Diana hadn't heard Blake struggle before on the racetrack. Blake's struggles drew Diana in as if she was inside the car with Blake, struggling with him.

Blake's masterful driving skills, indomitable will, and sound character saved the day. Race fans and commentators watching the race wouldn't have known of Blake's struggles. Blake missed no pit stalls, incurred no pit-road speeding penalties, and made no other driving or tactical errors. But Diana knew from the radio that Blake had to struggle mightily simply to do as he ordinarily did.

Although Blake started in seventh, he gradually fell back in the early parts of the race. He was outside the top ten at the conclusion of the first two stages, scoring no stage points. Most of the other playoff drivers picked up stage points, one of them, Blake's teammate, with a stage win.

But Blake didn't fall very far back. Indeed, that may have been the frustrating part of his race. Despite the team's tire pressure and suspension adjustments on nearly every pit stop, Blake's car ran no worse and no better than between tenth and fifteenth place. Nothing that Blake or his team did seemed to have any efficacy. They may as well have made *no* adjustments as having made the many that they did.

As a result, Blake was neither a factor nor a non-factor in the race. He just lurked on the margins of relevance throughout the race.

The last few laps typified the rest of the race. Nearly the whole field, other than the leaders, pitted on the last caution for fresh tires. Blake, running in twelfth place, joined the other cars.

When the race resumed, the first few cars with fresh tires jumped to life, overwhelming the leaders. Blake's car, though, wasn't among those cars that responded to the fresh tires. His car simply continued to run mundane laps, resulting in a thirteenth-place finish.

Only two playoff drivers finished behind Blake. Blake was already below the cut line. Not far below, but below.

Vegas had been a desultory if not disastrous race. Blake had struggled mightily with no particular effect, as if struggling in another realm.

5

Diana descended spritely from atop Blake's pit box as the race came to its end. She wanted to try to meet Blake's car on its way back to the garage, as she had done after qualifying.

Diana was enjoying more and more the sense of caring for Blake in his mood and emotions, although Blake still seemed to need or desire little such care.

Blake wasn't a needy person. Nor was Diana. But Diana was learning to appreciate the small opportunities she had to discern Blake's mood, to share in its depth and reflection.

Blake had a generally cheerful demeanor. He also had extraordinary equanimity. Diana could imagine that not even earthquakes could shake Blake.

But equanimity doesn't mean the absence of feelings and emotions. Blake wasn't emotionless, cold, unmovable. And Blake wasn't a cypher, hiding his emotions deep within himself.

Diana loved sharing in Blake's cheerfulness. Diana wasn't as cheerful as Blake. She didn't have a sunny disposition. She certainly wasn't negative or morose. But her circumstances tended to influence her mood more than she wished.

The opposite, though, was true of Blake. His circumstances seemed not to affect his mood at all. And Diana drew richly on Blake's steady light of positive sensibility.

So often, Blake's presence just instantly lifted Diana's mood, which she welcomed. Others might have stuck resolutely to their pessimism, turning away the cheerful one's buoying effect. But not Diana. Diana's spirit seized and drew on the energy Blake's bright disposition left in its wake.

Yet Diana also liked sharing in Blake's pensiveness. Diana hadn't really seen Blake despondent, down, or depressed. But Diana had seen Blake go through so many challenges over the course of the racing season that she had certainly seen him hard pressed. Blake responded to those circumstances with contemplative musing and readiness to reflect. Diana relished in that spirit, being naturally contemplative herself.

Diana hadn't yet detected in her relationship with Blake any contrary annoyance. Nothing about Blake irritated Diana. She supposed that irritations would in time come. Living with a spouse differs from courting and engagement. They don't call it a *honeymoon* for nothing.

But whatever irritations might arise between them, Diana could see that they would be small and quickly dissipate. Diana had found a compatible mate, when for some, compatibility is ninety percent of the challenge.

As Diana walked briskly up the lane from pit road toward the garage, Blake's car came into view behind her off pit road. Diana had timed it just right. Her heart made a small jump.

Blake slowed his car as it approached Diana's side. He already had his window netting down. As his car rolled up to Diana, Blake reached through the window to take Diana's hand and give it a squeeze.

Diana smiled at Blake deep inside the car. Seeing the pleasant squint of Blake's eyes through his helmet's visor, Diana imagined that Blake had smiled back.

Blake's car rolled on to the garage.

"Meh, right?" the crew chief greeted Blake after Blake had climbed from the car and removed his helmet outside the garage.

Blake shared a thin smile with the crew chief at his humor over their thirteenth place finish.

Blake leaned against a tool chest in the back of the garage, listening to his crew chief and race engineer analyze the race and results. Soon, the team was wheeling the car and equipment out to the hauler for its long trip home. Blake, the crew chief, and the race engineer remained, speaking quietly in the back of the garage.

The crew chief had his theories, most of them involving race strategy. The crew chief admitted that they might have missed some opportunities that other teams had discerned and seized.

Blake shook his head, saying, "Didn't seem so. You were right on throughout the race."

The crew chief scowled, wanting to take responsibility while wanting even more to believe in his ability to have influenced the outcome somehow.

The race engineer also had his theories, most of them involving car setups, track temperatures, tire pressures, spring adjustments, and track compound.

The race engineer had a hunch that they hadn't given Blake the car he needed and deserved.

Once again, Blake shook his head, saying, "No, I thought the car did fine."

The race engineer, like the crew chief before him, scowled for the same reasons, wanting to relieve Blake of concern while asserting the engineer's own efficacy. Rubbing his temples, the race engineer muttered that he'd go right back to work on it and have something new for Blake and the team to consider.

"Let's get home to figure it out," Blake suggested, adding, "I'm not alarmed. I've got a sense of what's going on."

The crew chief raised his eyebrows in interest. So did the race engineer.

Blake, though, had already turned away. Blake busied himself with gathering his helmet and gloves to pack away for the long trip home to Charlotte and on to Homestead Miami for next weekend's race.

Blake didn't want to debrief with the crew chief. Blake knew that his struggle had been in that higher realm, the one to which the yurt man had pointed. The ordinary, disappointing, but not imperiling race results were clearly not the fault of the crew chief or crew. The crew chief had done everything that crew chiefs know to do. The race engineer had given Blake a decent car setup, one that avoided a catastrophic crash while keeping the car within shouting distance of the leaders. And the pit crew performed admirably.

Nothing had failed. It was just that nothing had really worked.

In that sense, Blake knew that the yurt man had already proven prophetic. The yurt man had spoken of Blake's struggle on a higher plane, where the will and wiles of humankind have no direct effect. The yurt man had spoken of Blake emptying himself of human will and wiles, to discern the will and draw on the power of the one who, in emptying himself, had created the world.

Blake had rediscovered, embedded in the yurt man's revelations, the power of attention. As much as Blake wanted and needed to attend to racing things, like car setups and aero packages, he knew that to reach the championship level, he needed to attend to the profound, as the source of all rationality.

Indeed, to race with his full power, his entire concentration, attention, and right mind, Blake needed to connect with the deific, attending to the divine. Only with attentive listening to every prompt around, inside, and beyond him, would Blake restore his team's efficacy. Until he attended properly, nothing his race team did would influence the outcome. Blake's outcome was in the hands of another realm.

Blake, though, wasn't frustrated. He preferred that his struggle be in that other realm. Blake raced for that transformational purpose. Like the yurt man fleeing to the mountains, Blake inside his race car pursued his divine dream.

Each has a path to the divine, some through yurts or darkness retreats, while others through nursing, doctoring, lawyering, or accounting, and still others through marathon running or stock-car racing. The pursuit or race isn't the real thing. The real thing lies just beyond.

Blake was beginning to understand the championship, as the championship demands. The yurt man's partnership was already at work. The seeds of success had concentrated their form in a humbling thirteenth-place finish, when only concentration within a seed will bring forth the full flower of the greatest good.

As the song says, *old souls were rising again in a new world*. Ideals like a Cup championship beckon but also judge. The final round had judged Blake a thirteenth-place finisher, not against his playoff competition but against the championship itself. And so Blake embraced his humbling, knowing that to stand before the creator is not just to learn of one's shortcomings but to discern one's possibilities.

Blake thus knew that Vegas had been the perfect race with which to begin the final playoff round.

Blake was all smiles back at the team facility on Monday, bantering with the crew chief, race engineer, and mechanics as they dragged themselves in after the long flight home. The race hauler wouldn't arrive until early the next morning, when it would be quick turn-around time.

Later that day, Blake and the team's other three drivers met with the team owner in the owner's office.

The owner and drivers often did meet in the days following a race. The team owner wasn't in any sense a meddler. He would instead generally leave race strategy and tactics to the drivers and their crew chiefs, even though the team owner could have contributed much. If the owner had an idea, he would more likely raise it in one of his similar meetings with the four crew chiefs.

The team owner instead gathered his four drivers to ensure that they maintained the trust and respect of, and had the full benefit of the wisdom of, one another. The team owner seldom brought any agenda to the meetings with his drivers, although he might have some news about sponsors or other business developments. Instead, the owner just wanted to hear his drivers talk, evaluate their mood and attitude, and watch his drivers interact.

"Obviously, very happy with our results," the other playoff driver began, when the owner asked him how he was feeling.

"I mean, a stage win, and then a top-five finish," the playoff driver continued, adding, "I just felt that we were really on the money throughout the race. With a break here or there, we could easily have won."

The team owner nodded. Blake somewhat expected the team owner to turn to him next. Blake was the team's only other remaining playoff driver. But the owner instead turned to the other two drivers, one at a time asking how they felt.

"We did decent," the first driver said with a small shrug, adding, "The good thing is that we improved throughout the race. And we've already got some good ideas for Homestead Miami."

The owner nodded. The driver had started well back but finished just behind Blake.

The owner then turned to the other non-playoff driver.

"Same here, I'd say," the driver began, "Started well, got bottled up in traffic a bit, worked our way out of it toward the front. Finished top ten and could've been top five if it weren't for the late caution. Probably made the wrong call taking four tires rather than two on that last caution, but that's only in hindsight. Some of the others did, too, and it worked for some of them."

The owner once again nodded. Blake took a deep breath for his turn.

But instead of asking Blake how he was feeling, the owner merely turned to Blake, saying, "You good?"

Blake nodded without speaking, sensing that the owner didn't want to hear from Blake at the moment. And he was right. The owner quickly turned to a few housekeeping details. Sponsors loved Homestead Miami, so be ready to give them due time. He'd be going down later than usual to attend to other business. Call him if anything comes up.

The owner picked up some papers on his desk, as the signal that the meeting was over. The drivers rose to leave, joking happily as they did so. They knew that the owner wanted to see them supporting one another.

Blake paused at the office door, the others having already made their way out and down the hall. Looking back into the office, Blake saw the owner smile and give a tip of his head to Blake to return to the office and take a seat. Smiling back, Blake did so.

The team owner had a strong and close relationship with each of his drivers. The team owner strove to maintain those relationships, in part by treating his four drivers equitably. The parent who favors a child in front of the others does all the children a disfavor, sowing seeds of discord through jealousy.

Yet the team owner had a special relationship with Blake. The other drivers knew it and accepted it. But the owner was wise not to show it in front of the other drivers.

"You and that brother in law of yours have something up your sleeves, don't you?" the owner said with a sly smile, as Blake took his seat again across the owner's desk.

"You don't miss much, do you?" Blake said with a laugh.

"It's my business not to miss much," the owner agreed with a smile and nod, "But will you take a bit of advice?"

"From you, of course, always," Blake replied, adding, "You know you never need to ask."

"Just don't tell the other drivers what you're up to," the owner said.

The owner paused before continuing, "I'd never say that if I thought it would help them to know. But it won't. You're your own breed of cat, you know?"

The owner and Blake laughed together.

"Interesting way of putting it," Blake replied, still chuckling, adding, "And no, that cat's not coming out of the bag. It wouldn't help any of us if it did so."

Blake rose to go. But the owner cleared his throat to speak, just as Blake reached the door.

"Do you really think it will help?" the owner asked in all seriousness.

Blake paused before answering, "More than anything else, although we'll do everything else, too."

The owner nodded. Blake left, smiling to himself in appreciation for his team owner.

By the end of Monday, Blake and Diana had other good news.

Blake had agreed with Diana in Las Vegas that the Speedway Club at Charlotte Motor Speedway would be a fitting wedding site. Diana had also cleared the choice with her two driver's wife friends.

Marla had then undertaken the sensitive task of securing the reservation, when everyone knows that such things usually require a year's notice or more.

For whom is the reservation? the Club's wedding planner had grudgingly asked, surprised that anyone might think the Club would be available on such short notice.

We'll make the arrangements, the Club's wedding planner had replied, as soon as Marla disclosed the identity of the wedding party inquiring.

Diana and Blake had a perfect venue for a year-end, New Year's Eve wedding. The Club accommodated three-hundred guests. Diana and Blake now had the challenge of deciding the invites.

Three-hundred guests would ordinarily make for a good-sized wedding party. Not, though, for Blake and Diana. Simply inviting drivers, owners, and spouses, not to mention pit crew members, team staff, and track staff, could overwhelm the venue.

Diana and Marla decided to recruit Diana's two driver's wife friends to discern and execute a wedding-invite strategy. Their race was on, just like the final round of the playoffs.

6

"How about an after-wedding bash at the Fillmore?" one driver's wife proposed.

"Gosh, gal," the other driver's wife agreed, "That *would* be fun. And it would soften the blow of not getting a coveted invite. Doesn't the Fillmore hold around two thousand?"

Diana, Marla, and Diana's two driver's wife friends had arranged to meet over lunch on Tuesday. Although they had the wedding dress and venue, time was still of the essence. Invitations needed to get out, and for that to happen, they needed an invitation list. All four would be off to Homestead Miami shortly, where race events would keep them busy. They needed to work on invitations *now*.

Diana's party wasn't an issue. She had a few friends, her college roommate Julie among them, who would attend. The issue was instead the stock-car community, among which Blake had hundreds if not thousands of strong relationships. Drivers, owners, crew members, stock-car staff, track staff, sponsor representatives, media friends, and other categories each had dozens of invitation candidates. Where to begin, and where to stop?

That was when one driver's wife had suggested the Fillmore for a reception location.

"Go ahead and invite everyone who might have any claim for offense if you hadn't invited them," the driver's wife suggested.

Diana and Marla looked at one another.

"You know, Honey," the other driver's wife said, "Cost is not a consideration."

The two wives laughed. But Diana and Marla knew they were right. The point was to honor the community for its support of its members, not to have the biggest, most-expensive bash. Weddings, after all, can be better celebrations than funerals. They can also be better celebrations than championships. One of the wives drove home the point.

"If one of our husbands wins the championship, only one of us will be celebrating," she said, adding, "But for your wedding? Honey, we'll *all* be dancing away the night!"

The two wives laughed again. This time, Diana and Marla laughed with them.

Using her cellphone, Marla made a quick check of the Fillmore. It had no event scheduled for New Year's Eve. She made a quick call to confirm its availability. They'd need entertainment, but for that, they had a lot of good choices.

With the Fillmore's two-thousand-seat venue for a reception, their planning for the three-hundred wedding guests went more easily. They listed the categories and candidates within each category, and then ranked the candidates. The only question, then, was where to make the cutoffs in each category, to balance the invitations out.

"Looks like our work is done, Honey," one driver's wife said in satisfaction, adding, "You'll be revising the list a lot, working with Blake, but you're on your way."

The two wives rose, hugged Diana from behind in her seat, and departed. Diana watched them go, thinking that soon she would share their peculiar and prominent roles and status. A stock-car driver's wife. She'd never imagined it. Wedding preparations made it ever more real.

Blake was still thinking of his team owner's question, which had been whether Blake's consultation with the yurt man, indeed his acceptance of the man's proposal and partnership, would work in bringing Blake closer to the championship. Blake wanted to bring the question up again with Rob that Tuesday evening with Diana at Rob and Marla's residence.

Blake and Diana had met early that evening on the patio behind the residence. There, in the dwindling sun and settling cool, they had pored over the draft wedding-invitation list.

The list impressed Blake, who quipped in kind jest, "Plainly the work of geniuses."

Diana laughed.

Blake was aware of Diana's new friendship with the two driver's wives. He was also happy for Diana.

Blake didn't believe Diana to be like either of the driver's wives at all. And he was glad of that, although he liked and respected both of them. To Blake, Diana was unlike any of the driver's wives, and he hoped that it stayed that way. He also suspected many other drivers felt the same way about their wife, that each was unique and should remain so.

Yet Blake knew the challenges that a driver's wife faces. Driver's wife is in some ways a privileged role but in other ways an itinerant, shifting, and dubiously challenging role. Most professional athletes win about half the time. Stock-car Cup drivers seldom if ever do. And a driver's wife can bear the brunt of the emotional toll.

So Blake was glad to see that two driver's wives who had already successfully navigated and endured the transition had befriended Diana. He hoped that they would become sound counsel to Diana on a wife's challenges, if ever she needed such counsel. And Blake appreciated their wedding-planning gifts.

Blake and Diana settled on the bulk of the list, leaving margin for adjustments later. Diana already had offers for help with the design of the invitations.

Rob and Marla joined Blake and Diana for a light meal on the patio. As the evening cooled, Marla and Diana headed inside. Rob and Blake remained on the patio. Blake was eager to broach the yurt-man question.

Rob first pointed out to Blake that both of them had sufficient humility to seek and listen to the wisdom of others. Blake certainly listened to his team owner but also to Rob, Marla, Diana, Fred, and others. And Blake would listen to his crew chief, race engineer, spotter, and mechanics. Many counselors make for wise decisions, Rob reminded Blake, who needed no reminder.

They agreed then that the question wasn't of accepting counsel and insight. The questions were instead the peculiar nature of the one who in this instance was giving the insight, along with the different nature of the insight he gave.

Here, though, Rob suggested another bit of guiding wisdom, insight Rob admitted he drew from the yurt man himself.

"Fasten your seatbelt, Big Guy," Rob warned, knowing that he would also need to attend diligently to the conversation simply to get the idea articulately across.

"A Cup championship marks extraordinary success, of course," Rob began, adding, "But extraordinary success requires the ability to engage transformationally."

Blake thought for a moment before nodding and saying, "Doing the ordinary gets ordinary results."

"Precisely," Rob replied, "Although our friend might say instead that ordinary practice inevitably ossifies into rigidity."

Blake smiled in appreciation. Rob was indeed hard at work to convey the yurt man's idea precisely and articulately.

"The challenge with many extraordinary endeavors, a Cup championship pursuit certainly among them, is that the variables are so numerous that chaos will at some point rear its disruptive head," Rob continued.

Blake nodded again. His Las Vegas race hadn't been especially chaotic. If anything, it had instead been too ordinary. Perhaps a few wrecks, blown tires, blown engines, and pit road penalties sprinkled among the field would have helped. But a championship driver wouldn't wish chaos on his own team. And those bits of chaos had felled many teams' championship hopes.

"We typically use known and familiar means to attempt to quell chaos," Rob resumed, "When to the contrary chaos is chaotic because it has superseded those ordinary means."

Blake had to think for a moment for an example, before saying, "Like using the same pit procedures a hundred times until the hundred-and-first time those procedures fail in an inevitable anomaly the procedures themselves embedded."

"Exactly," Rob replied, glad for Blake's example. "And that's what happens to many playoff teams. The embedded anomalies eventually catch up to them."

"So how does one anticipate what by definition one cannot anticipate, or one would have followed better procedures?" Blake asked.

"You mean how does one thwart a demon one doesn't know?" Rob said with a smile.

Blake chuckled, admitting, "I suppose so."

"By appealing in advance to the superordinate order that subsumes as-yet-unexpressed chaos," Rob replied.

"You mean to appeal to the creator whose creation orders all chaos?" Blake asked.

Rob now had the occasion to chuckle, admitting, "Exactly so. Appealing to the superordinate order means moving up the creator's mountain nearer his home. It means perceiving the centralizing axis around which order congeals. It means embracing the proper, rather than the corrupt, animating spirit. Or it means conformity with the transcendent source, however one puts it."

Blake was silent. The stars, though, seemed to spark and call in the cool and darkening night. Finally, Blake spoke.

"And our friend may help us perceive the centralizing axis, animating spirit, and transcendent source?" Blake asked.

"We're all always trying to do that together, aren't we?" Rob replied.

Blake nodded. But he had another question.

"Why a man from the mountains outside Phoenix?" Blake asked.

Rob took a moment to consider how to answer.

"One doesn't draw the transformational from within the familiar," Rob said, adding, "One must sometimes move outside the boundary, finding the pearl in the depths or the gem in the mouth of the dragon. Our friend has moved himself toward the depths where he may just draw us up a great pearl."

"May I still use the simulator?" Blake quipped.

They both laughed. But again, Blake regretted having seemed to mock their yurt friend.

"Please tell him I said thank you," Blake asked Rob, who nodded.

Rob led Blake back inside to escape the evening's cold. Inside, Diana was ready to take her leave, needing a good night's rest. Blake showed her to the door, stepping outside in the cold evening to give her a goodnight hug and kiss. Blake would stay a few more minutes.

Rob, too, soon headed for bed.

Marla made Blake a mug of warm milk, an old habit they had shared from childhood. Neither was ready to retire. Each had too much in mind for sleep to entice them.

"You alright, Sis," Blake asked when they had settled down at the dining table with their mugs of milk.

"I'm alright," Marla replied, glad as always for Blake's brotherly concern.

"You're the best," Marla added.

Blake smiled, while looking down to toy with his mug. Blake was glad as always for Marla's kindness.

"I've been wanting to share something with you," Marla said after each had taken a sip from their mugs.

Blake looked up at Marla.

"With the wedding approaching," Marla resumed, "I've been planning a change."

Blake shook his head, still looking at Marla.

"No," Marla continued, "Diana needs to be doing what I'm doing for you. She'd be perfect, much better than I've been for you. She's a natural at everything I do only with labor."

Blake shook his head, now looking down at his mug instead of at Marla. He had anticipated this moment, but he wasn't happy at its coming, and he wasn't sure it was right.

"I have some things I've been wanting to do, too," Marla continued, adding, "So it's not a question of Diana just taking my place. She'd be freeing me to do what I should probably do."

Blake looked up at Marla. Marla was surprised to see Blake's eyes glisten.

"Would you tell me about your plans before you make any final decisions?" Blake asked.

"Of course," Marla replied, adding, "And I want to help you with Diana's transition, too. If it's alright with you, I'd like to speak with her sometime soon, maybe even in the next week or two if we can find the right moment."

Blake nodded. Reaching over to place his hand on Marla's arm, Blake repeated to Marla what she had just said to him, "You're the best."

They smiled at one another. Blake rose, gave Marla a hug, and headed out into the night.

Blake was back at the race facility early the next morning.

The race engineer had labored over car setups since their return from Las Vegas. Blake had spent a good part of Tuesday on the simulator, taking lap after lap around the virtual Homestead-Miami Speedway track. Those laps had given the race engineer the opportunity to run dozens of test setups, refining the choices. Blake would spend a good part of Wednesday on the simulator, too, adding more laps to the count.

As Blake let his muscle memory take over, searching for the tiniest adaptations that might produce slightly faster laps, his mind wandered to superordinate order.

Motor racing, Blake realized, had to be among humankind's most orderly endeavors. It wasn't quite a space shot, where precision measurements meant the difference between landing in the ocean or bouncing off the atmosphere and into deep space. But motor racing for hundreds of miles at hundreds of miles an hour along an oval paved track certainly required immense effort to maintain order while fighting the encroachment of chaos.

Blake thought of the tiniest things that could completely undo a playoff driver, from running over a hose in the pit stall, resulting in a pass-through penalty, to picking up a piece of track debris and cutting a tire. The least little parts defect, or the least little wrong twist of the steering wheel, and a playoff hunt might be over.

Rob was right. The yurt man was right. Ordinary efforts, indeed extraordinary efforts, though necessary, weren't enough to anticipate and avoid every crippling anomaly. The chaotic movement of time embedded anomalies in space, no matter how hard, smartly, and efficiently a race team tried.

Blake knew better than to give up. He knew better than to simply take his hands off the steering wheel. Superordinate order, the centralizing axis, wanted Blake's cooperation, indeed his submission and devotion. Blake had to learn more about how to try without interfering, how to strive without doing so out of his own means, which were fatally inadequate.

Somewhere on the umpteenth simulator lap, Blake arrived at a new peace with the superordinate order. The centralizing axis took hold, shaking out the chaotic kinks. And Blake's soul didn't rise in triumph but knelt in worship.

"That's good for today," the race engineer said to Blake, while looking yet again at a run of simulator data on the monitor in front of him.

"You feeling alright about it?" the race engineer added.

Blake smiled and nodded.

"Hey," the race engineer recalled, "Back in Vegas, you said you had an idea what was up with our inability to make any progress. Care to share your idea?"

"Oh, that's alright," Blake demurred, adding while pointing to the race engineer's monitor, "It's probably right there in the data."

The race engineer gave Blake a quizzical look.

Blake shrugged, smiled, and left.

7

"Our friend has a message for you," Rob said to Blake, adding, "Just got it this morning."

It was Thursday, time for everyone to head to Homestead-Miami Speedway. Blake's race hauler and motorhome had already left. Diana, Rob, and Marla would fly down together, while Blake flew down on the team owner's jet with the other three drivers.

Rob and Blake had met for a quick fast-food breakfast. They got their orders and took a seat in a booth by the window. Sunlight lit the plastic table.

"And the message is?" Blake asked with genuine curiosity, pleased that their curious friend was still invested in their championship partnership. Blake pictured their friend in his yurt, pounding out a message on a laptop computer under dim lights, barely powered by the solar panel's batteries.

Rob pulled his cellphone from his pocket, took a swipe at it, and began reading.

"He begins, 'Beware,'" Rob said, pausing for effect.

"Oh, boy," Blake said in light jest.

Rob laughed before resuming.

"'Beware in your appeal to superordinate order,'" Rob began again. He continued, "'Superordinate order does not mean ever-stricter order. Superordinate order is mitigated order. Rest in the creator balances and vitalizes superordinate order, letting it accomplish its rule over chaos."

Rob took a deep breath before concluding, "'To exacerbate order tyrannizes, opening the door for chaos.'"

Rob stopped.

"That's it?" Blake asked.

Rob nodded.

Blake thought for a moment before replying, "That's a riddle, right?"

Both Blake and Rob laughed.

"Could you read it again?"

Rob read the yurt man's message again. They each took a bite of their breakfast sandwiches. Finally, Blake spoke.

"You know, he's right."

Rob nodded but said, "Give me your application."

"Playoff teams often try to do more," Blake began, continuing, "They tighten every screw a little harder. They go over and over and over their routines."

"And?" Rob asked as Blake paused for another bite of his breakfast sandwich.

"And their effort to exceed what had been a sort of ideal order, the rhythm and routine that won them races and got them into the playoffs, becomes a tyranny."

"What do you mean, *a tyranny*?" Rob asked, although he knew exactly what Blake meant.

"Nerves fray," Blake began, continuing, "Then conflicts erupt, while team members miss the obvious adjustments they need to make because of their single-minded focus on a prior order. Their effort toward the centralizing axis, the creator's superordinate order, becomes an exacerbated order that invites and unleashes chaos."

"Hmm," Rob replied, "Good way of putting it. Rationality all the way down is tyranny and destruction. One must rise to and rest in the creator rather than attempt to take one's own flight. Or to put it the other way, the devil parades as an angel of light."

Blake raised his eyebrows, saying, "An even better way of putting it."

Rob consumed the rest of his breakfast sandwich in thought before asking, "Have you seen any evidence within your team of that exacerbated order?"

"No," Blake promptly replied, adding, "But given our friend's message, I suspect that we're about to see it."

Rob shrugged, saying only, "Let's hope not." But like Blake, he knew it was coming.

And they didn't have long to wait.

Blake was at the race facility minutes later. His crew chief met him at the door. One of their mechanics had quit. They'd be sending a backup to Homestead-Miami Speedway.

"Quit?" Blake asked. He couldn't remember anyone having just up and resigned from the race team before.

"He said he couldn't take it anymore," the crew chief explained, "Wasn't sleeping at night, things weren't good at home, just needed a break."

Blake shook his head, his thoughts instantly turning to the tyranny of exacerbated order.

"I told him to see HR, maybe get some counseling, and that we should just call it a respite or needed personal break," the crew chief explained, adding, "He's too good to lose."

"Good move," Blake said, shaking his head again, while adding, "Let's watch that we're not pushing too hard."

"Playoff run, Bud," the crew chief replied, "You know the drill."

Blake didn't reply. He'd made his point. If he had pressed the crew chief, he would only have been succumbing further to exacerbated order's demand. But his team had just lost a mechanic whom the crew chief had said was *too good to lose*. And that wasn't helping Blake's playoff run. Pushing too hard stirs chaos rather than quelling it.

Blake spent the next hour gathering his things, getting ready to depart on the owner's jet for Homestead-Miami Speedway. But in the middle of that hour, something nudged him to take a break to visit the logistics manager.

For Blake and every other race team member, the logistics manager was a daily hero. She made sure that every team member got where they needed to go, on time and with as little delay and disruption as possible. More importantly, she made sure that every team member got home in the same way.

The things the logistics manager did to accomplish her duties were not just airline, rental-car, and hotel reservations. They included ordering and sometimes even fixing meals for a crew delayed in transit, making emergency ride calls in the middle of the night, monitoring a pregnant wife's labor to ensure the husband gets home in time, and arranging police escorts.

Blake hadn't spoken with the logistic manager since the playoffs started, even though her office was not far down the hall. They chatted frequently during the regular season. Blake liked hearing about the exploits of her teenage children whom he had met on several occasions and tried to encourage. But the playoffs seemed to soak up so much extra time.

The logistics manager was, of course, in her office. She was always in her office, often early in the morning and late at night. Blake took a respectful glance through the office window before knocking on the door. As he did so, he noticed she was crying.

Blake hesitated but opened the door slightly anyway, just enough to say, "Hey, can I help?"

The logistics manager looked up, shrugging. With tears streaming down her face, she insisted, "I'll be alright. I'll be alright. How can I help you?"

But even as she asked, she sobbed again.

"No, no," Blake replied, "I'm not here for anything. I just wanted to say hi and see how you're doing. We haven't talked in a long while."

"I know, but it's been so busy around here," the manager replied, adding with another sob, "And people just don't seem to care anymore."

"Hey," Blake reassured her, "We care. But what's going on?"

"Just my teens," the manager said with a dismissive wave of her hand, "You know them. They're wonderful but always a challenge."

Blake could tell the manager didn't want to share the details. He looked at his watch.

"Look," Blake said, "I've got an extra half hour. How about if I swing by their school just to say hi?"

The manager's mouth fell open in disbelief and protest. She started to object, but Blake raised a hand gently to silence her.

"I've got an errand to run anyway," Blake said, "And its been too long since I've seen them. I'll only stay a minute. Just call the school, would you?"

The manager nodded obediently, still in disbelief. Blake began to close the door, but the manager called to him.

"Blake," she said, "I was about to quit. Thank you."

Blake shook his head, saying only, "Heroes don't quit. But we're going to take better care of you."

Blake grabbed a couple of souvenir T-shirts and caps on his way to the school. The manager's teens were waiting when he pulled up. Blake waved to them to jump in his car, where they chatted for the next few minutes.

"I'll check on you again soon," Blake said as he handed them the t-shirts and caps, and they got out of the car to head back to their classes.

Blake made a quick stop to pick up trip supplies before heading back to the race facility. On his way, he received a call from his crew chief. Blake tapped the hands-free screen on the dashboard.

"What's up?" Blake answered.

"Hauler's broken down," the crew chief replied, adding, "Everything will get there, but it'll be a bit of scramble, and we might see delays. Can't fix it on the road. We've arranged for a tow truck."

"What happened?" Blake asked, stunned. He'd heard of hauler breakdowns before, but they usually involved quick roadside repairs, with a delay of only a couple of hours.

"You'll never believe it," the crew chief replied, "But when checking and rechecking and rechecking the fluids after the long trip back from Vegas, someone left a cap off, and the engine fried."

"Weren't they watching the gauges?" Blake asked, incredulous.

"Strangest thing," the crew chief replied, "But the gauges evidently weren't reading properly. Something about maintenance also having swapped out a control board just to be sure it would work. Well, it was working, but the new board wasn't."

"Hard to believe," Blake replied, although he was instead thinking again of exacerbated order. They'd have been fine except for their extra efforts, the anomalies of which had ruined the hauler's engine.

Blake was back in his office at the race facility minutes later, hoping he'd heard the last of the chaotic workings. But his fun wasn't quite over.

The crew chief and race engineer knocked on his door, peering in its window. Blake nodded and waved them in.

"Um," the race engineer began as he and the crew chief stood inside the doorway, "We're going to have to redo the car's setup as soon as it gets to the track.

"Huh?" Blake asked, "Redo it?"

The race engineer nodded sheepishly while the crew chief scowled at him.

"I had the right setup printed and in my hands," the race engineer explained, "But I decided to print the three others that we were considering and compare them all one last time just to be sure. I must have picked up the wrong one when I took it over to the mechanics."

Blake shook his head, thinking again, *exacerbated order*. But then he laughed.

"You're the best," Blake said to the race engineer, "Always going over everything. Thanks, and don't worry about it. I'm sure the guys will have everything straight in no time."

Blake paused before adding with another laugh, "Well, as soon as the tow truck gets the hauler there."

The crew chief looked like he wanted to argue. In fact, the crew chief and race engineer had been arguing before they got to Blake's office. And Blake had noticed the crew chief's ire.

But Blake had felt a nudge not to exacerbate the order even further with recriminations over the anomaly that exacerbated order had already created. That's what demons do, Blake mused, remembering something the yurt man had said. They foster chaos, and then use the chaos to promote more chaos until chaos floods the plain.

The yurt man's insights had helped Blake see what he had long known. The influences of order and chaos pull in opposite directions. And they do so parallel to time and space. Chaos works in circular time, while order works in solid space.

But the yurt man's message had also warned that the goal isn't to crush chaos with perfect order. Creation leaves a seventh-day remainder for restoration and rest. And that remainder, outside the bounds of work's order, is where creativity refreshes order.

"Come on," Blake said to the race engineer and crew chief, "Let's get out of here and get to Homestead. I have a feeling something good is waiting for us there."

The race engineer and crew chief looked at one another, puzzled. They both shrugged. They then both laughed. The crew chief clapped the race engineer on the shoulder, as they turned to leave. Blake picked up his packed bag and followed them out the office door.

Diana was already at the motorhome parked on the grassy infield of Homestead-Miami Speedway when Blake rode up in a golf cart with his traveling bag. She threw her arms around his neck and gave him a great hug as he stepped from the cart with his bag.

"Heard about the hauler breakdown," Diana said quietly.

Blake smiled and shrugged, saying, "Just another small bump in the road."

"Am I a bump in your road?" Diana asked playfully, her arms still around Blake's neck.

Blake laughed while shaking his head.

"So maybe I'm your providential shipwreck instead?" Diana tried again.

Blake thought for only a brief moment before saying, "You haven't yet looked like any shipwreck to me, although you're certainly providential."

Blake gave Diana a squeeze about the waist with his free arm, while his other arm still held his traveling bag.

"Oh, I'm a broken vessel," Diana warned him playfully, "But even a broken vessel can be a gift in its repair."

Blake laughed. They kissed, Diana still holding Blake tight.

"Come on," Diana finally said as she loosened her grip around Blake's neck, "Let's get you to the garage and to work. You've got a championship to win."

"You know," Blake said, "They've still got setup to do. And they've got to redo the car's setup, too. How about if we take a walk for a bit?"

"I'm all yours," Diana replied, giving Blake another kiss.

Marla was already at work inspecting the corporate hospitality suites, unpacking items and materials, and going over her lists of corporate representatives to greet.

Rob helped Marla get her materials to the suites and then headed off to meet with his security team.

Diana loved these times at the racetracks when teams and staff were arriving and setting up, before the racing began. As she and Blake strolled the grounds, they waved to acquaintances who had, like them, traveled a long way to gather yet again at another beautiful racing venue. They stopped here and there to chat with those acquaintances. Everyone was busy, but a relaxed busy, when most everyone was more than willing to stop for a chat.

The race schedule's weekly gatherings and departures fostered the sense of family that the racing community shared. Family members depart and rejoin one another in daily and weekly rhythms that the family members come to treasure. Both the departures and the gatherings play their role. Getting away from family is important, too. But gathering again is the greater part, as Blake and Diana's stroll proved.

Their stroll ended at the race garage, where Diana and Blake parted with another kiss. Diana lingered outside the garage to watch Blake work with his team. Although they were in the midst of the playoff's final round, Diana marveled at Blake's joy and levity. Nothing seemed to consume Blake, not even a playoff push. To Diana, Blake always bore a sense of riding above the things at hand. Blake kept an inward eye on the mountaintop.

As Blake worked with the crew chief and mechanics inside the race garage, Diana wondered outside where the mountaintop would next lead.

8

Race day dawned clear, unseasonably warm, and typically humid, a perfect South Florida morning.

Blake's race hauler had arrived in tow. The crew had set up the garage quickly. And the race engineer had gotten the car in its proper setup, so good that Blake's practice runs were at the top of the board.

Qualifying went just about as well. Blake qualified in the second row. He might have won the pole but for a slight wiggle and lift just before he came out of the last turn, stealing the tiniest bit of speed from his lap time. Blake had spent the evening before Sunday's race at the garage as usual, watching the mechanics inspect and clean the car, and listening to the crew chief and race engineer discuss strategy and tactics.

Rob met Blake at the motorhome early, just after dawn, where they sipped coffee, lounged, and chatted. Marla and Diana made their way to the motorhome not long after. The four of them relaxed, chatted, and laughed together in the motorhome's security, in one of those timeless moments that families treasure.

"Time to get to the garage for one last review?" Rob finally asked as the morning wore on. He was reluctant to break the spell.

Blake, though, had another idea.

"Chapel's about to start," he said as he rose from his seat, adding, "Let's spend a little more quiet time together there."

Blake took Diana's hand, helping her rise. Rob and Marla followed Blake and Diana from the motorhome.

The ministry Motor Racing Outreach, formed to help racing families in crisis, held a quiet mid-morning reflection for drivers, crew, and their families on most race days, usually at an infield tent or track meeting room.

Blake didn't ordinarily attend. Racing was usually his full focus on race days. But the yurt man's message and events since had reminded Blake of the balance he needed to hold.

Blake, Diana, Rob, and Marla took seats in the back row. Prayer, quiet song, and quiet words of encouragement followed. Diana thought of her coming wedding and how she hoped that her marriage would reflect the marriage of the creator and his fellowship bride. Rob thought of the health and safety of everyone who would gather at the track that day. Marla thought of the community of Blake's supporters whom she would soon welcome.

Blake would ordinarily have thought of the coming race. But this one morning, he thought instead of the worship that he felt going on around him.

Blake might have thought of how good taking this short while to reflect and refresh would be for the race, the day, or the week. But instead Blake reached into worship's prerational, pre-instrumental, premoral heart.

Blake didn't worship that morning with a purpose, not to invoke the creator's protection nor for blessing, healing, proximity, or a race win. Thinking of the yurt man's wisdom, Blake instead worshiped without request, simply attending to the pinnacle so far above him.

And in that moment, the pinnacle drew a straight line through him, ordering his spirit, soul, and convictions aright, without any tyranny. No emotion rose or fell. No word came forth, and no thought congealed. Nothing touched or overwhelmed him. Blake just attended to the hierarchy's top.

Shortly later, Blake was at the garage reviewing things with his crew chief, race engineer, and spotter. Marla had headed for the corporate suites. Rob was making the rounds of his security detail.

Only Diana lingered behind at the infield tent, renewing acquaintances while making new friends.

Diana noticed one of her two driver's wife friends sitting alone. Diana had noticed her husband head to the garage, like Blake. Diana assumed correctly that she was now at loose ends, at least until the race started.

"May I join you?" Diana asked, motioning toward a seat beside the lone driver's wife.

"Hey, Darling," the driver's wife said, "Sit down and tell me how it's going. Invitations out yet?"

"First round on their way," Diana reported dutifully with a smile.

The driver's wife gave Diana a high five, saying, "You're just about all hooked up," as she did so.

Diana laughed, saying with a smile, "Sure am."

Both women took a deep breath, hoping to enjoy a few more minutes of quiet before the big race day. They chatted amiably as they sat.

"You're atop the pit box for the race?" Diana soon asked.

"My spot, Honey," the driver's wife replied, adding, "We'll see if I can last the whole race."

"Does it tire you?" Diana asked, adding, "I mean, I'm still experiencing races differently. And I never quite seem to know how I'll react."

The driver's wife looked kindly at Diana before replying.

"Yes," she replied, "I know what you mean. Sometimes I feel like a race fan, jumping up and down, rooting him on like crazy. But other times, the whole race just seems to pass by with my spirit or soul in another place."

Diana nodded, saying, "Exactly. Good to know I'm not crazy. And good to know I'm not alone."

Diana touched her friend's arm. Her friend put her hand on Diana's.

"Well, Babe," the driver's wife said, "Looks like it's getting to be time for the big show. 'Driver's start your engine,' huh?"

They both laughed as they rose.

Hours later, Diana was atop Blake's pit box. The drivers were in their cars, rolling off pit road.

As soon as Diana settled into her seat behind Blake's crew chief and race engineer, she felt the building excitement of the race. Instantly, she knew she would experience the race as a fan, not as a distant soul. And she was glad for the excitement. It had already been a good day, and goodness would see the day through.

"Any last words?" Blake's voice came over Diana's radio headset.

"Hah," the crew chief laughed in reply, "You'll be hearing plenty more of them."

"You ready up there, Billy?" Blake called to his spotter high above the grandstand.

"Got sunscreen on my arms and legs, and my straw hat on!" Blake's spotter Billy replied.

"Tell Cliff I'm beating his boy, fair and square today," Blake joked with Billy who, Blake assumed, was standing next to the spotter for a favorite competitor.

"Oh, he's right here, and I've already told him!" Billy replied.

"Alright you knuckleheads, pay attention," the crew chief chided in jest.

Diana smiled at the pre-race camaraderie she heard over the radio. She hoped it would last. The crew chief turned and gave her a thumbs up, acknowledging the good spirits. Diana gave a thumbs up back with a broader smile.

The cars were indeed completing their warm-up laps and beginning to assemble in their qualifying rows, two by two. Shortly, they were bunching up in the tight starting pack. And then, they were gaining speed in unison to roar past the grandstand under the waving green flag.

Diana picked out Blake's car in the second row, tight behind the car ahead of him.

The race was exciting from the start. Some races unfold slowly, packing the excitement toward the end. Not so, this race. Cars competed from the start.

Blake held his position in the top five for the first several laps. But just when the drivers began to sort out their positions to settle in for the first stage race, two drivers tangled around one of the curves. One car slid up the track and into the outside wall. The race had its first wreck in the first dozen laps.

The first stage held other excitement, including multiple lead changes, an engine failure bringing out a caution to clean fluids from the track, and strategic green-flag pit stops. Diana watched the race, breathless with excitement.

Blake and his crew chief weren't playing it safe, either. Diana could tell from the tense radio chatter that they were making judgment after judgment on racing lines, tire pressures, and the timing of pit stops.

Billy the spotter was doing his work, too. Time after time, Billy had a call for Blake just as Blake needed it, keeping Blake clear of debris and wrecks, and clearer of racers with bad cars, bad attitudes, or bad intentions.

Blake's race engineer also seemed furiously at work atop the pit box, in front of Diana and beside the crew chief. He was making and relaying calculations, checking competitor data, and testing scenario after scenario at the crew chief's command.

Their coordination and work enthralled Diana, drawing her deeper into the world and spirit of racing than she had been before. Diana had until then largely observed races as a new fan. Homestead-Miami Speedway's intense playoff racing helped her to experience racing as a veteran fan or even a team member. Indeed, for the first time, Diana was beginning to feel like a part of the team.

Blake's team had always welcomed her, treating her kindly and with respect. But she had nonetheless felt like a guest and outsider. She didn't know much of how the team worked, and she played no part in its working.

But watching the racing at Homestead-Miami Speedway, Diana suddenly felt like she was ready to take part. She wouldn't be a race engineer or a car mechanic. She wouldn't drive the hauler or mount the spotter stand with binoculars to call the racing like Billy. Yet Diana sensed that she was ready to join the team in a capacity fitting to her skills and talents.

In all, the Homestead-Miami race proved to be racing at its best. The race held excitement from start to finish. Blake mostly held his position in the top five or ten, except when cycling through green-flag pit stops. Other racers, though, fell way back and yet with lucky dogs, wave arounds, and bold driving made it back near the front.

The racing repeatedly drew the crowd to its feet.

Blake, still within sight of the leaders, grabbed a few points at the end of the first stage, as the cars flew under the green-checkered flag.

Blake's crew chief had more small adjustments to make on the car, during the pit stop under the stage end's caution. Blake's pit crew nonetheless held the car's position as Blake came off pit road. But predictably, some cars had pitted in the last few laps before the stage's end. Those cars remained on track under the stage end's caution.

Thus when the field emerged from pit road after the stage end's caution, Blake found himself roughly in the middle of the pack, among the other speedy cars that had won stage points.

The shuffling of the field at the stage's end produced yet more dramatic racing. Blake and most of the other drivers who had been at the pack's front for stage one gradually raced their way back to the front. In the course of doing so, though, their efforts offended some of the slower drivers whom they passed.

The offenses didn't immediately result in obvious payback. Stock-car racing had cleaned up some of the more obvious acts of retaliation with penalties imposed during the regular season. No racer wanted a suspension at the end of the year that might interfere either with the playoffs or championship race.

But the offenses did result in greater intensity of the racing. Drivers with slower cars were even more reluctant to give up track position to faster cars. And drivers with faster cars felt compelled to take even more aggressive action to get past them.

Stage two thus brought two more wrecks, the first involving two cars and the second involving three. Pit crews managed to patch together two of the five wrecked cars. Those two patched-together cars, limping around the track while shedding debris, further increased the peril and excitement of the racing.

Intensity that had begun at level five on a scale to ten and that had reached seven or eight by the end of stage one jumped to nine by the end of stage two. Once again, though, Blake flew under the green-checkered flag at the end of stage two, having gained more stage points.

Diana wanted to breathe a big sigh of relief and relax as Blake and other leaders came down pit road under the stage end's yellow caution. But just like at the end of stage one, cars that had pitted just before the end of stage two remained on the track. And Blake's pit crew had to battle to get Blake back out on the track near the front of the pitting leaders.

Diana had no chance to catch her breath. The pit stop, if anything, further increased the excitement. The race's intensity seemed to remain at a ten out of ten for the rest of the race.

Blake's pit crew once again got him back out on track near the front of the pitting leaders. But those leaders were now in the middle of the pack, behind more than a dozen other cars on the lead lap that hadn't pitted. And once again, that meant that Blake and the other drivers of the faster cars that had earned stage points would have to race to the front, once again producing predictable offense.

Unsurprisingly, the final stage brought another, bigger wreck involving five cars, only one of which was able to limp back out on track after extensive pit-road repairs. Diana finally caught her breath while the pack circled the track behind the pace car and track crews cleaned up the debris and fluids from the big wreck. But soon, the racers were flashing under the green flag restarting the race's final stage.

The final stage brought several more up-and-down battles, with drivers of fast cars falling way back due to pit strategy or small correctable issues and then hurtling their way forward near the front once again.

Blake, though, held his position near the front once he had regained that position after the end of stage two had reshuffled the pack. Blake's spotter Billy kept Blake out of trouble on the track, while Blake's crew chief and race engineer timed the pit strategy perfectly. Diana watched Blake's colorful car hurtle around and around the track for the rest of the final stage, always near the lead.

A great race's end must somehow top the dramatics that occurred through the course of the race, and this great race indeed did. Two of the lead cars had gained their track position by gambling on fuel strategy. Race fans, commentators, and pit crews held their breath as those cars careened and then sputtered, and then slowed, and then stopped on the track, out of gas. The crowd moaned in sympathy and regret as the caution flag came out just before the final lap.

None of the leaders pitted during the caution, while track cleanup vehicles pushed the two out-of-gas cars back to pit road. The pace car soon pulled from the track, unleashing the pack to gradually build its speed until its mad dash out of the restart zone. The pack flew under the green flag, still with two laps to go.

As the race pack flew around the first banked turn, Blake was in fourth place, on the inside or lower lane behind one car, with two cars on the outside or upper lane surging ahead of them. Cars behind jostled one another rudely in fruitless attempts to gain positions. Somehow, none wrecked.

The field made it all the way around again to the white flag, leaving just one perilous lap to go. The drivers all somehow held the pack's fury together around the first curve and back straightaway, until the pack dove into the final great turn. At that moment, the pack exploded apart in a spectacular wreck affecting every car except the four cars in front, which continued down the front straightaway and toward the checkered flag.

Blake's car flashed under the checkered flag in fourth place. Two of the cars ahead of Blake were also playoff drivers. But Blake had earned enough points that he was now solidly above the playoff cutoff, with only one race to go in the final round, Martinsville, before they all headed to Phoenix for the championship race.

9

"We've got another message from our friend," Rob told Blake as they settled into the plastic booth at the fast-food place where they were grabbing a breakfast sandwich.

It was late Monday morning after the Homestead-Miami Speedway race. Blake had made it home on the owner's jet with the team's other three drivers. The mood on the trip home was good, now with both Blake and the team's other playoff driver above the cut line.

Rob, Marla, and Diana had also made it home.

Blake's race hauler had even made it back overnight, although pulled by a different tractor. The hauler's own tractor still needed its engine replaced.

"What does our friend have to say?" Blake asked Rob while preparing for his first bite of the sandwich.

Rob pulled his cellphone from his pocket, gave it a swipe, and started to read, "'Beware....'"

Rob paused. Blake laughed.

"Here we go again," Blake said, adding, "Last time, he was dead on."

Rob resumed, "'Beware the remainder. As a circle has six parts and an irresolvable seventh-part remainder, the week entails six days of routine with a seventh-day encounter with the unknown.'"

Rob paused, letting Blake digest the preamble. He then resumed.

"'The remainder is both the devil's tail and the saint's redemption, the potential out of which the creator draws life while also the chaos out of which demons draw demise. The remainder is the frill on a skirt and the gargoyle leering over the precipice.'"

Rob paused again before concluding.

"'Do not begrudge the remainder's adornment nor fall prey to the remainder's allure. Submitting to the remainder drowns one in chaos, while attempts to vanquish the remainder meet their chaotic fate.'"

Rob slid his cellphone into his pocket and took a bite of his sandwich.

"Another riddle, for sure," Blake admitted, shaking his head, adding, "Are you up to a paraphrase?"

"I've had a bit already to think about it," Rob replied, "So I'll give you a hint. What's a circle's circumference?"

Blake thought only for a moment before answering blankly, "Pi times twice the radius. Or, if you prefer, pi times the diameter. Why?"

"Well," Rob began to answer, but Blake cut him off.

"Wait, don't tell me. I've got it. Pi is a little more than three. So a circle has six radiuses plus pi's remainder. But pi is an irrational number, meaning that one cannot calculate precisely the value of that remainder."

Rob smiled, saying, "You're good at riddles."

"Not really," Blake replied, "Our friend spelled it out for us. I just had to get it in my head."

Both were silent for a moment, enjoying the refreshment of their sandwiches. Blake soon resumed.

"I do like that he's drawn a parallel between pi's irrational remainder, which is also the irrational seventh remainder of a circle, and our Sunday day of worshiping the indefinable creator."

"But our creator isn't irrational," Rob objected.

"No, he's not," Blake agreed, continuing, "Nor is he entirely unknowable. He makes himself known in sufficient part. Yet we don't observe directly the realm he rules. And he's not alone in that realm, where both obedient and disobedient spirits dwell."

Rob thought for a moment, trying to draw out the point. He finally said, "So that remainder realm is both necessary as the source of life yet perilous as a source of deception."

Blake nodded, saying, "Something like that, as far as we can express it. We draw both potential and peril from the remainder, that foreign land outside our bounds."

Rob finished his sandwich. So did Blake.

"Application, then?" Rob asked.

"Oh, I think our role is first to recognize the remainder," Blake guessed, "And then to distinguish whether and what to draw from it."

Rob nodded, adding, "And don't forget the part about not trying to rid ourselves of remainders."

Blake nodded, saying, "Right. That might be the most important part. Everything has boundaries. They are necessary to life. But that also means everything has remainders, foreign entities lurking outside the bounds. And those foreign entities aren't always enemies. They may at times instead be sources of life."

"Or *something like that*," Rob repeated Blake's earlier acknowledgment with a smile.

Blake laughed, saying, "That's the beauty of riddles. They're purposely only loosely defined."

They both rose, disposed of their remainders, and headed out into Charlotte's bright, chill sunlight.

"Thank him, will you?" Blake called to Rob as they each headed for their cars. Rob nodded and waved.

Martinsville week offered a different rhythm for the race teams still in the playoff hunt. First, Martinsville Speedway is only a little more than two hours north of Charlotte, where many of the teams had their race facilities. That meant a lot less travel time eating up the week.

Martinsville's proximity to team facilities also meant that at least some race team members could commute. No air travel, no rental cars, no hotels, and instead sleeping in one's own bed at night. Martinsville thus offered something of a respite week before the sport's hundreds of workers traveled far out west to Phoenix for the championship week.

But Martinsville also offered a completely different racing challenge than the drivers and teams had faced in well over a month, since Bristol in mid September. Martinsville, like Bristol, is a short track, indeed, even shorter than Bristol. The cars, setups, maneuvers, and strategies would all differ from any of the ovals and the superspeedway and road course on which they had raced recently.

Martinsville wasn't exactly a wild card like Denton International Speedway or Talladega Superspeedway. It wasn't pack racing, pushing one another around the track at ridiculous speeds and in absurd proximity. But Martinsville was different enough to inject yet another level of playoff uncertainty.

Blake, his crew chief, and the race engineer spent all Monday working on race strategy.

Late in the day, though, the team owner called the four drivers in for their meeting. The four drivers took their seats on the other side of the owner's vast desk, which the owner had adorned sparsely with racing memorabilia.

"So how are you feeling?" the owner asked Blake first.

Blake smiled, thinking of their last meeting when the owner hadn't even asked.

"Looking forward to Martinsville," Blake said simply, neither with a note of arrogance nor a note of jest.

One of the other drivers guffawed, saying, "Martinsville wouldn't be the choice of many playoff drivers trying to preserve their championship hopes."

The other driver still in the playoff hunt remained silent, almost grim. What the other driver had said was indeed true. Martinsville close racing made it easy for drivers to influence or even control the race's outcome for other drivers. A bump here, a block there, a spin around the corner, and out go those championship hopes.

Blake just continued to smile. He was already thinking of Martinsville as a remainder race, the little tail that could wag the big dog. Martinsville was the indefinable last playoff race before the championship. It was such a short little racetrack, around which the drivers nonetheless would take a ridiculous five-hundred loops, that it had its own irrationality. It was the pi race that would reduce four drivers to irrelevance while exalting four others to the championship race.

All day in his strategizing with the crew chief and race engineer, Blake thus resisted the thought either of succumbing to Martinsville's short-track allure or attempting to fully vanquish its wiles. Each time the crew chief proposed a unique strategy to dominate and eliminate Martinsville, Blake rejected it. But each time the race engineer proposed a contrary strategy to account for each of Martinsville minute quirks, Blake likewise rejected it.

What Blake wanted to do was to draw from Martinsville's absurdity, its quirky nature so foreign to stock-car ovals, without giving in to it. In a sense, Blake wanted to race Martinsville like any other track, maintaining the team's spirit and identity, while incorporating enough of Martinsville into the team's spirit and identity to broaden and deepen both.

Of course, Blake said none of this directly to his crew chief or race engineer. And he breathed no word of it to the other drivers at the team owner's meeting.

"How about you?" the owner asked the next driver, and then the next driver.

Neither driver was in the playoff hunt. But both drivers shared their impressions, each of them satisfying the owner that they remained committed to the team's overall cause.

Finally, the owner turned to the other driver in the playoff hunt.

"Could you and your crew chief stop by my office around ten tomorrow morning?" the owner asked him.

The driver nodded.

"Thanks, guys," the owner said to the four of them, adding, "You know where to find me. It's going to be a good week."

Blake couldn't help noticing the puzzled, even alarmed, look on the other playoff driver's face as the four of them rose and made their way to the door. Blake also noticed that none of them were showing any signs of the jocularity they had shown as they left the owner's office the last time. They were all thinking of the owner's request to meet with the other playoff driver and crew chief.

The team owner cleared his throat just as Blake was about to step out of the office behind the other drivers. Blake paused to let the other drivers disappear down the hallway. Then he turned and stepped back into the owner's office. The owner motioned Blake back to the seat he had just abandoned.

"Something up your sleeve again, huh?" the owner asked, smiling slyly at Blake.

Blake nodded with an even bigger smile.

"Your yurt man was right last time, wasn't he?" the owner asked.

Blake nodded.

"Figured so," the owner said, adding, "The race results pretty much showed it."

"That's it?" Blake asked, starting to rise from his seat.

"No," the owner said. Blake settled back in his chair, puzzled.

"Tell your brother in law I'd like to meet your yurt man. At Phoenix. After you win the championship."

Blake smiled, nodded, and rose quickly to leave. But he paused at the door.

"He may not be comfortable," Blake said, adding, "And he may not be who or what you expect."

"That's why I'd like to meet him," the owner said.

Blake smiled again, nodded, and left.

Tuesday passed without a major event, to Blake's relief. No news spread of what the team owner might have shared with the other playoff driver and his crew chief.

That evening, Blake and Diana met at Rob and Marla's residence, as usual. It was too cool for the patio, so they had their light meal inside. Rob and Blake retired to the den while Marla and Diana lingered over coffee and the remainder of a chocolate dessert.

Soon, Marla broached the subject she'd already brought up with Blake.

"Honey, I've been exploring some plans," Marla began.

Diana looked up from her coffee.

"Nothing's firm yet," Marla continued, "Because I need you to help me make a decision."

Diana reached across the dining table to place a hand on Marla's forearm. Marla smiled kindly at Diana in return.

"I don't want to leave you with something you'd rather not do," Marla said. "Hard to believe, but the season ends after next week. I'm not sure I want to return in the same role next year. We both know you'd be perfect for it, far better than me."

Diana waited for Marla to continue. When she didn't, Diana spoke.

"Only if you truly had something calling you," Diana said, adding, "You're perfect for Blake, and I'd never take your place if you had any desire to continue."

Marla shook her head, saying, "No, I'm not feeling that desire."

"But what's calling you?" Diana asked.

Marla hesitated. Diana waited, not wanting to press. Finally, Marla spoke, slowly, unsure of herself.

"Rob and I need something," Marla began, "And we're not sure just what, yet."

"Any possibilities you've seen?" Diana asked.

"Too many," Marla laughed in reply. She paused before adding, "Things as far apart as starting a race team in a lower series, adopting a child, or fostering teens."

"Those all sound like wonderful ideas," Diana said sincerely. She paused before adding, "And not mutually exclusive, either."

"Thanks, Honey," Marla replied.

They each sipped their coffee, letting their thoughts settle. Finally, Diana asked what she felt might be the most important and helpful, but also the most sensitive, question, one that she almost dared not ask.

"Does it have to be apart from Blake and me?"

This time, Marla reached across the table to place her hand gently on Diana's forearm.

"I don't know," Marla answered, adding, "I think Rob and I are waiting to hear that answer. We love the two of you so deeply, and we would give our lives for your happiness."

"You already do," Diana said, looking down at her empty coffee cup in her hand. But she then looked up at Marla, adding, "And maybe that's the one thing that needs most to change."

"What do you mean, Honey?" Marla asked.

"If we don't find ways to elevate and free you and Rob, we will grow apart," Diana said.

Marla tipped her head in curiosity, wanting to hear more. Diana complied.

"You two give so much to Blake and now also to me," she explained, continuing, "That it wouldn't be right, natural, or healthy for it to last, for any of us. But what if we found a way to live and work and care for one another together, that had more balance to it in the ways that we love, serve, connect, and relate?"

Marla was nodding, nearly against her will. She knew Diana was right. She just hadn't wanted to hear it yet. But she also knew that she and Rob needed to hear it, and needed to hear it from Diana more than from Blake.

The two were silent again until Marla spoke.

"This is going to be good, isn't it?"

Diana smiled and nodded.

"We don't know what it is yet," Marla concluded, "But it's going to be good."

The two women rose, walked around the table, and hugged.

"Shall we find our guys?" Marla asked.

"Lead the way," Diana answered.

"I feel like playing a simple, silly, crazy game," Marla said as they headed for the den.

"I'm in," Diana replied.

Blake instantly recognized the silly board and card games that followed that evening, as the remainder's joyful refreshing, drawn from the deep well of potential the two women represented and held in trust between them.

10

"What are your plans for the extra time?" Blake asked his crew chief the next morning.

The hauler drivers and rest of Blake's crew had all day and much of the next day to pack the hauler to send it on its way to Martinsville, when the hauler would already have left if the race had been far out west.

"I'm going to have the crew empty everything out of the hauler that we've been lugging around all season," the crew chief replied, "And then put back in only the things we'll need for Martinsville. They've got the remaining time."

Blake shook his head. He didn't want to question his crew chief or interfere, but he was thinking of the message about what to draw and not to draw from remainders, including unexpected tails of time.

Blake also saw the hauler's accumulated detritus, those things that the crew would cast aside as unnecessary for Martinsville, as remainders. And those remainders just might be the key to a good run at Martinsville, even though the crew judged them today as waste and foreign to their efforts.

"How about if I get the stuff for a cookout here at noon for the crew and anyone who wants to join us?"

Blake instead proposed, adding, "Let's leave the hauler alone until the end of the season. We can clean it out then."

The crew chief scowled at Blake briefly but then shrugged, saying, "Yeah, they'd probably appreciate the time to unwind before the last big push. Go for it. Need a hand?"

"I've got it," Blake replied with a smile.

A moment later, Blake was on his cellphone.

"Hey, Honey, are you busy?" Blake asked Diana.

Satisfied with her reply, Blake proposed, "Would you like to help me put on a cookout for the crew at noon today? I'd meet you at the store in a half hour. We'd just bring everything back here and use the grill the guys keep out back. Nothing fancy."

Diana was in, with only one question. Diana wanted to know if she should invite Rob and Marla.

"Sure," Blake answered, "Of course, give them a call."

Diana did invite Rob and Marla, but both of them declined. And Blake wasn't disappointed. He had hoped that he and Diana would get to enjoy their time together alone, treating the crew.

The cookout was a hit. Blake hadn't seen his crew members enjoy themselves like they did that afternoon in months. He had almost forgotten their laughter and smiles around the race facility.

Diana enjoyed it, too. Blake had long wanted to see Diana with a role in which she was a part of the crew, rather than merely adjunct to it. To Blake, Diana appeared to enjoy bantering with the crew.

Blake also noticed that Diana took the opportunity to sit and chat with nearly every crew member, two or three at a time. Blake deliberately let Diana do so alone, although a couple of times he stopped to listen in. And sure enough, Diana was asking politely about spouses and children at home and off-season plans.

Diana needed to know those things to feel that she knew the crew. And the crew needed to know that Diana knew those things and cared about them, too.

"Time to get them back to work?" the crew chief asked Blake after an hour.

"No, let them enjoy it as long as they wish, even all afternoon," Blake replied, adding, "We've still got tomorrow morning."

The crew chief scowled briefly, so Blake added, "Anyone who has something they need to do can go but rejoin us when they can."

The crew chief's scowl disappeared.

Blake thought for a moment before reaching in his pocket, pulling out a credit card, and saying, "And here, send Billy over to buy more refreshments. He'll know what to do."

The crew chief raised his eyebrows, saying, "You know, this could get out of hand."

"I hope so," Blake replied with a sly smile.

The crew chief shook his head but headed over to Billy, who was busy regaling a table full of crew members with stories of a spotter's woes.

The first hour, only Blake's crew participated. In the second hour, members of other drivers' crews began drifting in. Blake sent Billy to the store for more provisions to restock the grill.

By the third hour, most of the crew members from all four crews were hanging out around the grill. Crew members had brought more chairs and folding tables out from the race facility to sit in the crisp afternoon's sun, moving them out of the shadows to catch the sun's warmth. The gathering had worked its way inside the race facility, too, as crew members carried Billy's refreshments inside to enjoy them in the building's warmth.

Somewhere in the middle of the afternoon, Blake saw the team owner making the rounds from table to table. Just as Diana had done, the team owner sat and chatted with twos and threes, catching up on family news. And Blake noticed Diana join the owner, walking beside him, listening, and laughing as he made those rounds.

Right about then, someone tapped Blake on the shoulder. He turned to find the other playoff driver, scowling like Blake's crew chief had scowled.

"Do you really think this was a good idea?" the driver asked, shaking his head in disbelief.

Blake just shrugged, not wanting to stir conflict with an answer.

Not satisfied, the driver clapped Blake on the shoulder with one hand while saying, "It's stuff like this that kills a championship run."

The driver turned and left.

Of course, Blake hadn't liked the driver's interference, although Blake understood that he might have interfered unintentionally with the driver's own crew.

But the driver's clap on Blake's shoulder had incensed Blake. He was glad that he had held his peace. He thought, though, of asking the team owner about the driver. Then, he remembered the owner's private meeting with the driver and his crew chief.

"Hey, Bud," a voice said to Blake from behind.

Blake turned to see the grinning team owner.

"Great idea," the owner was saying.

Blake smiled back with a nod, saying, "Seemed like the right thing." But with his smile fading, Blake added, "Although not everyone agrees."

"Don't worry about him," the owner replied.

The team owner had seen the driver's exchange with Blake. That's why he had come over.

Blake gave the owner a puzzled look, inviting the owner's explanation.

"Yeah," the owner explained, "That's why I met with him and his crew chief yesterday, for a little *coaching*, let's say, about team unity in a playoff run. Doesn't look like he got my message."

Blake looked off, not wanting to fuel a dispute.

"Don't worry about him, though," the owner continued, adding, "But just to be sure, I think I'll just sit atop his pit box this Sunday at Martinsville."

The owner let a broad, mischievous smile spread across his face. Blake remembered that the owner enjoyed, rather than got irritated by, the intrigue. So Blake smiled back.

"By the way, was this *outing* your yurt man's idea?" the owner asked as he turned to go. The owner had paused at how to describe it, especially now that it looked to be getting well out of hand.

Blake nodded, clarifying, "His inspiration, my application."

The owner smiled and waved as he drifted off into the crowd, slapping crew members on the back and laughing with them. Blake guessed that the owner wanted the *outing* to get out of hand that afternoon.

No sooner had the owner walked away than Blake's crew chief walked up, pointing at his watch.

"Our appointment with the open-wheel guest?" the crew chief was reminding Blake.

Blake looked at his watch. Indeed, he was to meet the visiting open-wheel driver in the next ten minutes. Blake hurried off, following the crew chief.

Blake had been looking forward to the open-wheel driver's visit. Blake had met him before. They both drove for the same owner. But Blake hadn't had a chance to talk with the open-wheel driver about racing. And that was what they had planned for the late afternoon.

As Blake headed to the reception area where they would meet the open-wheel driver, Blake thought how neatly the yurt man's insight into remainders, boundaries, and foreign encounters described Blake's visit with the open-wheel driver.

Stock-car racing has its boundaries, just as open-wheel, Formula 1, and other racing series have bounds. Relatively few racers drive in both open-wheel and stock-car racing, and when they do, it's typically only for a race or two. A stock-car driver is in a foreign land at an open-wheel event, beyond usual professional boundaries.

But Blake knew from his own experience driving an open-wheel racer in the Illianapolis 500 that drivers can learn when exploring across those boundaries. An open-wheel driver who tries to drive a stock car like an open-wheel racer will lose. Vice versa is also true. But a stock-car driver who finds in an open-wheel run a clue or two about racing in general may drive a stock car better than the stock-car driver who never tries an open-wheel run.

Blake was going to patrol that border cautiously. He wasn't going to draw the wrong things from his encounter with an open-wheel racer's foreign remainder. He wasn't going to spoil his keen stock-car driving skills with tactics that would only work in open-wheel racing. But Blake was going to learn and draw what he felt might rejuvenate, inform, and potentially transform his stock-car driving.

To Blake, that seemed to be the yurt man's insight. Blake was going to draw from this remainder, this extra bit of time stolen during Martinsville week from the usual travel, whatever might refresh his stock-car skills.

Blake and his open-wheel driver friend began their visit with an insider's tour. Blake showed the driver the offices, simulator, gym, and other spaces, equipment, and tools that Blake and the team's other three stock-car drivers daily used. As they toured, the open-wheel driver confirmed their common practices but also remarked on their different practices, giving Blake some insight into what he might want to adopt or adjust.

They spent a good part of the visit, though, at the simulator. Blake had already spent part of Tuesday and

Wednesday on the simulator, setup for Martinsville. Blake would get more simulator time the next morning before heading to the track. As Blake sat in the simulator running Martinsville laps, he described for the open-wheel driver what he was doing and seeing, while the open-wheel driver shared his reactions and insights.

Blake learned a couple of tips about sight lines along the car and track, and beyond to visual markers in the distance, things that the open-wheel driver used to gauge racing lines and braking zones. But Blake also learned some things about his own driving, just from his effort to describe his own driving to the open-wheel driver.

That double insight, Blake discerned, is the nature of encounters with the foreign, from which we both appropriate material and confirm or reject material of our own that we already hold.

Blake and the open-wheel driver also spent time in the race shop, looking over Blake's car. They each sat in the car, describing things to one another like windshield glare, pedal distances, seat support, harness interference, steering wheels, gloves, and shifters, that they felt, saw, used, and experienced. And once again, Blake learned from both the open-wheel driver's description and his own description of what he already knew.

The facility visit ended with the open-wheel driver's invitation to visit his race facility outside of Illianapolis, a visit Blake relished.

Blake and the open-wheel driver then headed to a local restaurant where they had arranged to meet Diana and the open-wheel driver's girlfriend for dinner. The two women were already there when Blake and the driver arrived. Diana looked resplendent.

For Diana, the dinner company was an unusual treat. Diana had in the past weeks enjoyed the friendship of her two drivers' wives. What Diana had not done was to spend any significant social time in the company of another driver and a girlfriend companion.

Diana knew well that the interpersonal dynamics for a girlfriend, fiancé, and wife differ. Diana had so far successfully navigated her way from girlfriend to fiancé, soon on her way to wife. Diana enjoyed the evening's opportunity to assess her own experience with Blake against that of another couple in an earlier stage of that natural progression.

Before Blake and the open-wheel driver arrived, Diana had already learned from the driver's girlfriend that she and her driver had not yet discussed engagement and marriage. Diana had barely introduced herself, when the girlfriend had already clarified her status.

Diana felt more than a twinge of sympathy for the uncertainty of the girlfriend's position. Diana learned, again without asking, that the driver and his girlfriend had been together for a year. The girlfriend gave no hint of where she felt the relationship might head. But Diana detected more than a hint of the girlfriend's wanting to know. Indeed, the girlfriend made it clear with a single quip that the girlfriend had for some time wanted to know the driver's intentions.

Diana later had a small chuckle to herself over how quickly and casually women can communicate such things to one another. Diana had barely known the girlfriend for five minutes, standing in a restaurant's reception area, and yet she already knew more about the girlfriend's relationship status than the driver would disclose or Blake would learn all evening.

Women share quickly and discreetly. Men learn only what they need to know, later.

Diana enjoyed the girlfriend's company throughout the dinner. Diana could see why the open-wheel driver would value her companionship. She was fun and funny, carrying the conversation when necessary, without dominating it. The open-wheel driver was shy, withdrawn. The girlfriend filled the void with the opposite.

Diana nonetheless got to hear from the open-wheel driver some of his own ambitions, challenges, and even fears and concerns. Diana hadn't expected it. She had assumed that Blake and his driver friend would keep things on the surface. But the driver's introverted personality seemed to draw those interior disclosures out of him. If he was going to speak at all, it would be about personal things rather than the topical things his girlfriend shared and enjoyed.

Diana treasured the insights she drew from the driver's disclosures of ambitions, challenges, fears, and concerns. Those disclosures gave Diana a picture of what Blake experienced. Blake didn't have the open-wheel driver's severely introverted nature. And so Blake wouldn't have naturally shared such an interior view of himself. But Diana could see that Blake must feel some of the things the open-wheel driver felt. Diana would keep those things in mind in the future.

Diana and Blake stood together for a few minutes outside her car in the restaurant's parking lot after the dinner, debriefing over the day while enjoying its richness.

Diana reached over to tousle the hair hanging over Blake's collar at the back of his neck, saying, "Need a haircut before the season's big finish?"

Blake looked into the night sky.

"No," Blake mused, thinking once more of the yurt man's insight, "Hair is an adornment, a remainder. I think I'll just let it go until after the championship."

Later that week, as he leaned on the tool chest in the back of his race team's Martinsville garage, watching his crew work on his car, Blake felt that it had been a perfect week, informed and guided by the yurt man's generous insights.

11

"Let's try to keep the car clean," the crew chief intoned over the race radio to Blake, adding, "Clean as you can, anyway."

"Roger that," Blake replied, "In this bumper-car merry go round."

"Half mile of mayhem," the crew chief corrected Blake, using the nickname the track's own president had coined.

Blake had used a sound analogy, though. Fitting more than forty race cars on a half mile track makes them look like a merry go round, once they space themselves relatively evenly around the tiny track.

Until they do, though, a Martinsville race pack looks more like a train steaming after its own caboose or a snake striking at its own tail.

Practice and qualifying had gone fine for Blake. His crew had seemed more relaxed and in its groove, Blake speculated because of Wednesday's impromptu cookout. Hangovers from that event had worn off by the time the crew reached the track late on Thursday and early on Friday.

Blake had again qualified near the front. He had no immediate concern about getting trapped in the depths of the pack. He was starting on the inside of the third row, in fifth position.

The team's other playoff driver had not fared so well. He had wrecked in practice, an egregious error for a late-playoff contender. The wreck was just bad enough for his crew to have to bring out a backup car. His crew chief and engineer hadn't found the right qualifying package. The driver was starting near the rear.

Diana was atop Blake's pit box. Marla was at her usual place in the corporate suites, even busier with sponsor representatives than usual, given the track's proximity to Charlotte and that Martinsville was the second-to-last race of the year. Rob was somewhere around the track, doing his security work.

Diana thought that the team owner might join her atop Blake's pit box, as he had done on a few other race occasions. But Diana had seen the owner mount his other playoff driver's pit box nearby, as the owner had let Blake know he planned to do.

The cars had assembled two by two in their tight pack, ready to snake swiftly around the track. The pace car dropped from the track down pit lane. And the pack gained speed into the start zone, where it roared off. The vast crowd circling the track stood and roared.

As she had done in the past few races, Diana quickly took note of her own mood. No, she wasn't a fan for this race. But no, she wasn't floating far above the track in her own world, either. And she wasn't in the car with Blake. *Ah*, Diana reflected to herself, *I'm a team member.* She smiled to herself over her new status.

The crew chief and race engineer atop Blake's pit box in front of Diana seemed busier than usual throughout the race. Like Diana, they repeatedly turned in their seats to follow Blake's course, and the course of the other drivers and cars, around and around the track.

Diana felt as if she was in the middle of a whirlpool, its pull turning her around and around in her seat. At times, she had to sit still and close her eyes to briefly tamp down the vertigo. But the whirlpool would quickly gather her once again as soon as she opened her eyes. She could not resist turning around and around to watch Blake's whirling progress around the track.

Blake remained near the front throughout the first stage, even briefly taking the lead in the middle of the stage. Diana heard from the radio chatter back and forth among Blake, the spotter Billy atop the grandstands, and the crew chief that Blake appeared to have neither short-run nor long-run speed but speed balanced across each run. That had been Blake's preferred strategy. Things appeared to be going well.

The same was not true for the team's other playoff driver who had started near the rear. Throughout the first stage, the other playoff driver fell further back until he was trailing the pack. Before long, the leaders had caught the other playoff driver, ready to put him a lap down.

Drivers hate going a lap down. But at Martinsville, many do. It's a Martinsville rite of passage.

On a larger oval track, trailing drivers might understandably resist the passing attempts of the race leader, especially near the end of a stage, to stay on the lead lap and bunch up behind the leaders again on the yellow caution.

But Martinsville is such a short track, with such short lap times of around twenty seconds, that a fast lead car can catch the back of the pack in not that many laps. A trailing driver has very little justification for blocking the leaders as they come up behind, especially when the race isn't near a stage end. Grudges and retaliation aside, trailing cars ordinarily let Martinsville race leaders through, pulling up the track or staying low on the track, out of the racing groove.

The other playoff driver from Blake's team, trailing the field, dutifully let the first race leaders pass, putting the driver a lap down.

Laps down at Martinsville aren't fatal to a driver's race as often as they are at other tracks. Drivers can get laps down back through lucky dogs and wave arounds on cautions. And Martinsville has more cautions than other tracks, averaging more than a dozen and sometimes seeing as many as fifteen or sixteen. That's the nature of short-track racing, producing more bumps, slides, wrecks, and cautions.

The other playoff driver from Blake's team thus wasn't by any means out of the race. He and his crew chief and crew just needed to make some smart adjustments, the sooner the better. The driver wasn't in a hopeless position, not yet even in great peril, instead just at a significant disadvantage he needed to correct fairly quickly.

Yet as Blake approached the rear bumper of the other playoff driver from his team, the other driver remained stubbornly in the racing groove. The other driver did not move up or down the track to let Blake pass, as the driver had let other race leaders pass.

Cars began to bunch up behind Blake, and the race leaders began to pull away ahead of Blake, as Blake stalked the other driver's car for an opportunity to pass. As Blake did so, he grumbled to his crew chief. The crew chief told Billy to ask the other driver's spotter what was up and to give Blake the break the other driver had given the race leaders.

But nothing changed. Indeed, the other driver not only remained stubbornly in the racing groove but actively blocked Blake up and down the track.

The other driver's racing would have been usual, expected, between competing drivers near the end of any stage or the end of the race. One might have even seen similar moves from a teammate in an especially important race. But not at this stage, not between these drivers, and not in this race.

For a moment, Blake's anger rose to the point that he resolved to nudge the other driver's car out of the way. Doing so would have risked a spin and wreck of the other driver, potentially costing the other driver a place among the four drivers who would compete for the championship in the next and final race.

But just as Blake had reached the boiling point, he thought for an instant of the yurt man's remainder. Was this odd, early race anomaly a remainder? If Blake wrecked his team's other playoff driver, would Blake have succumbed to rather than drawn from the remainder?

Blake patiently followed the other driver yet again around the track. One car, then two cars, slipped by Blake and the other driver in the process. Blake nonetheless remained patiently behind the other driver's car until, at last, the other driver gave Blake a deliberate opening. The other driver stuck a hand out his window in acknowledgment as Blake flew past.

Blake took a few laps to process what had just happened. But he soon concluded that somewhere between Billy's intercession atop the spotter stand and the instruction of the team owner atop the other driver's pit box, word had gotten through. Blake learned later that he was right on both counts. Yet for the moment, Blake was relieved not to have fallen into the remainder's trap.

The first stage concluded shortly later. Blake picked up a few stage points as his car flew under the green-checkered flag.

The first stage's end did not significantly reshuffle the pack. Pitting under green at Martinsville just isn't generally wise. Anyone who does runs the peril of going more than a lap down. So when the caution flag followed the first stage's end, the whole field made for pit road.

Blake's pit crew went furiously to work, including making a very small adjustment Blake and the crew chief had discerned. They would make no big swings throughout the race, only incremental adjustments. And most of those adjustments were to anticipate changing track conditions, not to correct any issue with Blake's car. Blake's car ran well all race.

Blake held his position coming out of pit road. Blake would start sixth for the second stage, on the outside of the third row.

As the cars reorganized themselves on track after the first stage's pit stop, warming their tires up and down the track to ready themselves for the restart, Blake's team owner descended from atop the other playoff driver's pit box. The owner walked down to Blake's pit box, peering about Blake's crew chief and race engineer.

With a big smile, Diana, sitting behind the crew chief, waved the owner up. The owner nodded with a return smile, made his way slowly up the pit box ladder, and took a seat in the back row beside Diana. The race engineer handed back a radio headset for the owner to don. Diana patted the owner's thigh excitedly, giving him a thumbs up. The owner gave a thumbs up back.

Communication atop a pit box during a race involves facial expressions and hand signals. The roar of the passing cars prevents much more, except occasional words shouted in the ear of an immediate neighbor who is momentarily willing to lift the protective headset from the ear.

The second stage proceeded for Blake much as the first stage had done. He moved up and down only a position or two or three throughout the stage.

This time, though, when Blake and the other race leaders began to lap cars at the back of the field, Blake experienced no unusual resistance. Indeed, when Blake reached the bumper of his team's other playoff driver, ready to lap the driver, the driver promptly pulled up the track to let Blake through.

Better yet, the driver pulled back down the track behind Blake, blocking other leaders behind Blake. The drivers behind Blake who had been fighting to pass Blake fell back, leaving a comforting gap behind Blake. Blake's intra-team opponent had somehow become his teammate ally. And Blake was pretty sure he knew why.

Blake's team owner, now watching the event unfold from atop Blake's pit box rather than the other driver's pit box, smiled to himself at his other driver's newfound courtesy.

Two cautions interrupted the second stage. Blake's crew chief ensured that Blake followed the few race leaders just ahead of him, pitting both times but taking two rather than four tires one time. Blake thus held his position among the race leaders. The race leaders had to fight their way back to the front through the few cars on the same lap that did not pit during the cautions. But doing so on fresh tires took only a handful of laps.

The second stage, like the first, went just about as well as Blake and the crew chief could have hoped. Blake flew under the green-checkered flag at the end of the second stage in fifth place, once again gaining a handful of stage points.

Once again, the full field, other than two laps-down cars, came down pit road under the second-stage caution. And once again, Blake's pit crew made the tire change, filled the gas tank, and made the small advised adjustment with their usual precision. Blake departed pit road still in fifth place.

The pace car soon pulled down off the track, unleashing the pack to its whirling fury. Under the green flag the pack flew for the long final stage.

It was during the third stage that Blake picked up on something that he had learned from his open-wheel friend on Wednesday. Blake's open-wheel friend had reminded Blake in their simulator time and discussions in and around Blake's car, how acutely aware of their sight lines and surroundings open-wheel drivers were during a race.

Blake had sensed that awareness in his practice, qualifying, and racing for his victorious Illianapolis 500 earlier in the year. But on Wednesday, his open-wheel friend had shown him some specifics of that awareness.

Blake's open-wheel friend had given Blake a new appreciation for how a driver's acute vision ahead out of the car, and acute sensations within it, can help a driver make the smallest adaptations to conditions, without the driver even necessarily knowing it.

The open-wheel driver's insights had reminded Blake of one of his odd yurt partner's insights shared on their first peculiar meeting at Las Vegas. The yurt man had spoken of pre-intellectual intuition and pre-instrumental judgments that a person's spirit makes from its proximity with the creator's spirit at the mountaintop.

Blake hadn't understood the insight at the time. But inside his race car, as he ticked off third-stage laps with ever-greater precision, Blake began to see that he wasn't thinking and judging. Rather, he was just driving, while his senses and spirit somehow attuned themselves not just to everything going on around him but also to the guidestar organizing those conditions for him.

Other drivers charging their way around Martinsville's short track that afternoon may have scoffed at Blake's brief insight. Stock-car racers don't always have to maintain that super-subtle, pre-rational awareness. Stock-car racing, especially at a bull ring like Martinsville, can involve more bumping and banging than precision driving. Calculated aggression, not superlative precision, is a stock-car racers trade.

But even at a bull ring like Martinsville, a stock-car racer can benefit from running precision lap after precision lap. Going five-hundred times around the tiny oval means that the smallest gain on each lap can translate into a huge difference at the end.

Blake's preconscious awareness had orchestrated those tiny gains. By the time the end of the third and final stage neared, Blake was in second place. Better yet, the top three cars were well out in front of the field. They had the race to themselves, if no yellow caution interrupted them.

Martinsville is notorious for late-race cautions. With so many opportunities for racers to bump and bang their competitors out of the way, Martinsville late-race cautions carry an air of inevitability.

But with the three race leaders so far in front, fewer competitors had any cause for forcing a caution. The three race leaders were also all among the eight playoff drivers fighting for a spot among the four drivers who would qualify for the championship next week at Phoenix.

Indeed, the crew chiefs of each of those three race leaders assured their drivers that they were in the championship, warning them against any rash action going for the race win. The second-place Blake and the third-place driver close behind him would only be risking their own harm if they fought hard for the Martinsville race win.

The checkered flag thus flew without further race drama. Blake finished second, right behind the race winner. Both of them, and the driver right behind Blake, qualified for the championship. The only other driver also to qualify for the championship had won at Las Vegas.

The other playoff driver from Blake's team failed to qualify among those four drivers. Blake was the only driver remaining from his team still in the championship hunt.

12

"So, it's finally here," Rob said to Blake as they settled into a booth at the fast-food restaurant Monday morning, "Championship week."

Blake smiled and nodded.

They each took a bite of their breakfast sandwich.

"Any word from our Phoenix friend yet?" Blake asked.

"Funny you should mention him," Rob replied with a broad smile, "But yes, although not what you might expect."

"Really?" Blake replied, "What did he say?"

"He wants to come to the race," Rob replied, "The championship race."

Blake laughed, saying, "So we've made a stock-car fan of the yurt man?"

"Well, I'm not sure he's a fan yet," Rob replied, joining in Blake's laughter, "But he's willing to meet the team owner after the race. And he said he wouldn't mind attending the race."

"I assume you can arrange it," Blake said, adding, "But let me know if I can help."

Rob nodded.

"Did he say anything else?" Blake asked.

"Sorry, Pal," Rob replied with a sly grin, "But you're on your own this week. Think you can handle it?"

They both laughed at Rob's jest. But Blake had one last thing to ask.

"Tell him thanks, would you?" Blake asked, "I mean, for Martinsville. He was spot on again."

"Done," Rob replied with an appreciative nod.

They finished their sandwiches, rose, and left.

Blake was at the race facility early that Monday morning.

Blake's week looked about like his other weeks had. He'd spend Monday planning race strategy with his crew chief and race engineer, meeting with the team owner late in the day if the owner asked. Then he'd spend Tuesday and Wednesday on simulator work before heading to Phoenix on the owner's jet on Thursday. The big difference was only that it was finally championship week.

The crew chief also expected a usual week, except that it was finally championship week. He'd ensure the crew had the race hauler unloaded from Martinsville and loaded for Phoenix, ready to leave Wednesday for the thirty-hour drive west.

Blake had asked for the crew's help getting his motorhome to Phoenix, so some of the crew would ride out in the motorhome. The rest would follow on commercial flights on Wednesday or Thursday.

Blake settled into the crew chief's office. The race engineer sat beside him. The three of them took a collective deep breath.

"So it's finally here," the crew chief murmured.

The race engineer and Blake both nodded. No one wanted to be the first to speak. The championship's weight pressed down upon them.

"Want some more coffee?" the race engineer asked, pointing to the crew chief's empty cup.

The crew chief nodded, handing his cup over the desk to the race engineer who left down the hall to the coffee maker. The crew chief then fiddled with a pencil, spinning it around on his desk in front of him.

"Okay, Chief," the crew chief finally said to Blake, "What're your thoughts on race strategy?"

"Chief?" Blake said with a smile, teasing the crew chief, "I thought you were the chief."

"You know what I mean," the crew chief scowled, although he let a small smile spread across his face in appreciation for Blake's good humor.

Blake hadn't known what to expect that morning from his crew chief. The crew chief was usually full of ideas. Their professional interaction usually involved Blake rejecting or affirming the crew chief's many ideas and proposals.

But Blake knew that the championship race was a different animal. And Blake hadn't yet discerned what ideas or approaches his crew chief might favor for it. Blake could usually predict his crew chief's views about an upcoming race and its best strategy. Not, though, for the championship. And it was now looking like the crew chief had no ideas or approaches.

The race engineer finally returned with the full cup of coffee. Handing it over the desk to the crew chief, the race engineer said, "So, what've you two shared so far? I'm all ears."

Blake and his crew chief looked at the race engineer blankly.

"Nothing," the crew chief answered, adding, "We were waiting for you."

The race engineer looked back at both of them, shrugging.

Blake wasn't disappointed at this unusual beginning to their championship-race strategy planning. To the contrary, he was already discerning something about the championship race that he had not yet considered: the championship race was unique. The strategies with which they were familiar didn't apply.

Blake proposed that they work forward from that beginning. They would take each of their usual race approaches and discuss why that approach was not right for the championship race. From that parsing they should begin to get a clearer idea of the championship approach.

"Think that'll be enough to come up with a winning strategy?" the race engineer asked.

"No," Blake said frankly, "But I've got a few other ideas."

"Care to share them?" the crew chief asked.

"No," Blake replied with a friendly smile.

"I didn't expect so," the crew chief replied with a chuckle.

The three of them spent the rest of the morning going through common race strategies, picking them apart as inappropriate for the championship. Play it safe? No point. In the championship race, there is no tomorrow. Win at all costs? Not exactly. One bold move invites retaliation.

Make friends? Not much point with the race ending the season. Proactive rather than reactive? But one needs a target, a point. Reactive rather than proactive? Better to dictate than to be dictated to. Don't beat yourself? But you still have to beat the championship competition.

Race the track? Better to race the competition. Race the competition? Better to consider the track's changing conditions. Race against the clock? The clock doesn't win the championship. Crossing the line ahead of the other championship drivers is what counts.

On and on they went, racking their brains for every strategy they could recall, while dissecting each strategy's faults for a championship race. By morning's end, they had exhausted every thought.

But they had also reached some conclusions, like *no driver counts except the other three championship drivers*. And *do nothing to impede another driver who isn't racing for the championship*. And *win the race, win the championship*. But *beat the other three drivers, and you win the championship, so you don't have to win the race*.

From their exhaustive investigation, Blake, his crew chief, and the race engineer decided on a novel strategy: they wouldn't have one. Instead, their strategy would be to monitor and then trump the strategies the other three drivers deployed.

Blake, his crew chief, and the race engineer discerned that the championship race is the one race where one can and should focus primarily or even solely on the competition. One cannot do so in the usual race because so many cars compete. But when only three other cars matter, focusing on the strategies those cars deploy becomes not only possible but potentially fruitful.

The crew chief hadn't been entirely convinced. But Blake asked him, *can't you tell pretty quickly what another team's strategy is?* Yes, the crew chief had replied. And *don't you generally know how to counteract that strategy?* Yes, the crew chief had replied. And *doesn't it frustrate you when another team counteracts your own strategy?* Yes, the crew chief had replied.

Then, Blake concluded, *don't let them know you have any strategy to counteract.* And instead, *counteract every little and big thing they do.*

Blake had convinced both the crew chief and race engineer. The two of them set about developing a list of common strategies they expected the other championship teams to attempt, and how to counteract those strategies.

Two tires? Four tires? Gas only? Don't pit? Pit early? Pit late? Pit with the leaders? Pit without the leaders? Lead? Follow the leader? Race hard early? Race hard late? Protect track position? Protect the lead? Short-run speed? Long-run speed? Race loose? Race tight? Speed into the turns? Speed out of the turns? Work the groove high? Work the groove low? Let others work the groove?

Blake's crew chief and race engineer listed every conceivable tactic and strategy, while discerning how best they could respond.

By mid-afternoon Monday, they had called the spotter Billy in to examine their list. From the spotter stand, Billy would help them discern the other three championship drivers' tactics and strategies. By late-afternoon Monday, they had called the other engineers and analysts in to examine their list, too. The other engineers and analysts would monitor the race data for the same reason, to help them discern what the other three drivers were doing.

By the end of Monday, Blake's crew chief was confident that they had a viable championship-race strategy, maybe even one that was uniquely viable.

That long strategy session Monday morning wasn't the only thing Blake did, though.

Blake spent Monday afternoon reaching out to everyone he knew whom he thought might help him confirm the best championship-race strategy.

Blake's first call was to his open-wheel friend, who congratulated Blake for making the championship final four. Blake gave his open-wheel friend due credit for Blake's Martinsville success. The rest of their brief conversation tended to confirm the direction Blake had discerned that morning.

Blake made call after call, to driving school instructors who had taught him long ago, mentors who knew little of driving strategy but much about Blake, retired drivers who had helped Blake along, past champions and Hall of Famers, former owners, and retired crew chiefs.

In doing so, Blake learned more about championship-race strategy, although nothing he learned significantly changed what he had concluded that morning.

But in making his many calls, Blake accomplished much more than confirming his own championship strategy. He also got to thank those to whom he owed thanks, apologize to those whom he owed apology, forgive those to whom he owed forgiveness, and encourage those whom he owed encouragement.

At a deeper level than just renewing, affirming, and restoring significant relationships, though, Blake also put his figurative house in order, something Blake had determined to do since that first night he met his yurt friend.

Common wisdom is that the creator doesn't answer the prayers of the unrighteous. But Blake had discerned from the yurt man's brief revelations that first night that unrighteousness doesn't just mean clumsy and obvious wrongs. It instead means any misalignment with the creator's patterns and principles, anything out of its hierarchical order, anything that points the person in a direction other than up the mountaintop of meaning or down into the creator's material chaos to carry that meaning's clarifying blessing and order.

When determining to make calls that afternoon regarding championship strategies, Blake hadn't even intended to clear his decks of unfulfilled obligations. He hadn't intended to realign relationships in their proper order. Blake's purpose had instead been instrumental, even selfish, to improve his championship chances.

But after the first few calls, Blake realized that his calls had a greater inherent value than their instrumental purpose. Blake was sharing his time, life, and love with people who had meant a lot to him. And he was sharing his time, life, and love precisely when those people might instead have expected him to be most selfish, to focus solely on the championship.

Blake also hadn't planned to make his last call of the day. He had only realized that he needed to do so, as he realized the greater value of the calls he had already made. The last person Blake dialed was his father.

Blake hadn't spoken with his father in years, not since well before Blake had become a successful stock-car driver. Blake's reason for keeping to himself, away from his father, had been sound. The wrong Blake's father had inflicted on Blake and on Blake's sister Marla warranted their full break from him. Blake's father had paid for that evil, while Blake and Marla had healed in the best way that children, both youthful and adult, know how.

But for the first time since their break, Blake felt that the time was right to make the call.

"It's Blake," he said simply and steadily, without either kindness or anger, in reply to his father's answer.

No words passed between Blake and his father that had any special consequence. They each spoke appropriately, as if from some universal script drafted for such painful occasions.

It was good to hear one another's voices, they agreed. The past had included awful wrongs, for which the wrongdoer deserves no forgiveness but somehow receives it anyway, in beseeching it. One was sorry and needing forgiveness, while the other was granting it generously without request. The pain would remain, though, perhaps for a long time, perhaps for a lifetime. Neither expected happy times with the other, but they both hoped for at least a relationship. And the call was over.

As Blake sat in his office, tears streaming down his face, he felt no particular sorrow for himself, although much for his sister Marla. Blake instead discerned that all are children of an atrocious tyranny, ruled by an inevitable death. In that sense, Blake cast no more blame on his father than the false angel of light whose enticement brought about that death.

But Blake simultaneously discerned that the greatest good comes only from confronting the greatest evil. Stare one's greatest harm in the face long enough and boldly enough, and you will reach your catharsis. That is the creator's promise in bidding the mortal to look on his son's cross to receive his son's immortality.

Blake wiped his tears to look down at the notes he had made of his afternoon's calls. Teardrops had stained and smudged those notes. He shook his head, trying to regain some sense of normalcy, of his willingness to stand to pick up again the challenge of the championship. And as he did so, Blake felt the challenge to be lighter than he could have perceived it. Indeed, Blake felt the championship challenge lifting him up rather than weighing him down.

Blake took a deep breath, stood up, and headed out the door to find Diana and get a bite to eat. He suddenly felt hungry and alive, like he wanted to rush headlong into the thrill of the coming week. And he thrilled even more to anticipate sharing the coming week with Diana.

Blake had finally and properly prepared for his first championship.

13

"Care to take a drive, Sweetheart?" Rob asked Marla.

Marla gave Rob a sly smile, saying, "Take me away, my love."

Marla, Rob, and Diana had arrived in Phoenix by commercial airliner earlier in the day on Thursday. Diana had already reconnected with Blake, who had flown in with the team's other drivers on the owner's jet.

The bright desert sun was just beginning to think about dipping below the mountains for the night. Rob and Marla probably had another hour to explore the environs by rental car before night fell. Both had completed their preliminary duties. Neither had an obligation for the evening. Indeed, their role was to stay out of everyone else's way until reassuming their duties the next day.

Rob turned the rental car eastward, away from the sun and toward the mountains. After a little while, Marla spoke.

"Are you looking forward to the wedding?" she asked.

Rob nodded, saying, "Are you?"

Marla nodded, too.

"What are you thinking?" Rob asked.

"I don't want to lose Blake," Marla answered.

"What do you mean, Honey?" Rob asked.

"I don't mean that he'll turn away from us in any sense," Marla replied. She continued, "He never would. Nor would Diana wish that he did so. In fact, I think the wedding will draw them both closer to us."

"Me, too," Rob agreed, adding, "So what do you mean about losing Blake?"

"I don't want us to turn away from him," Marla said, "Just because he's married."

Rob nodded.

"I know we'll give him and give Diana their space," Marla continued, adding, "I've already spoken with Diana about taking over my professional role with Blake, which I think would really help them share life as they should."

Rob nodded again. They drove on in silence for a few more miles before Marla resumed.

"You and I need something new," she said, "But not so new that it draws us away from them."

"What are you thinking?" Rob gently repeated his earlier question.

"I'm still thinking about a race team with Blake," Marla replied.

Rob raised his eyebrows. They had spoken together before about Blake's probable path forward, as his racing career matured. Other drivers had race teams in the lower series. Why not Blake? Blake would continue to drive for his team owner. He would just have his own small race team in the lower series, employing mostly new, young drivers, to grow as a leader, mentor, and manager.

But Rob and Marla hadn't discussed being a part of Blake's race team, if Blake indeed wanted to take that path.

"You mean you'd work for Blake helping him run his race team?" Rob asked.

"No," Marla replied, "You and I would own the team together with Blake and Diana. I'd manage the team. Blake would lead it and be its public face."

Rob smiled. He thought for a moment before saying, "I sort of like that, you in charge for a change."

Marla smiled back, saying, "I'd make a good boss, huh?"

They both laughed.

Rob took another moment before saying, "You didn't mention a role for me. Or for Diana for that matter."

"I don't know what you'd like to do," Marla said, putting her hand on Rob's shoulder as he drove, adding, "But Diana could handle the sponsorships and public relations, as she is going to soon do for Blake."

Rob took yet another moment before saying, "Let me think about it a bit. You know, we could always start a military security company together."

Marla laughed, saying, "Been there, done that."

Rob laughed with her.

They were now climbing into the mountains, through the shadows of the valleys and back out into the bright sun. Vegetation was increasing. Trees loomed ahead.

Soon, Marla spoke again.

"You know that Blake called dad?" she said.

Rob raised his eyebrows.

"It went alright," Marla continued.

"Are you alright that he did?" Rob asked.

"I think so," Marla replied. Her voice betrayed her uncertainty.

Rob took his turn reaching over to put his hand on Marla's shoulder. She looked back at him, put her hand atop his, and gave it a squeeze.

"Change is afoot," Rob said quietly.

Marla nodded.

As they ascended farther into the mountains, Marla asked, "Do you have a destination?"

"I was sort of thinking we might stop by to see a friend," Rob replied, adding, "But we don't have to do so."

"Let's do," Marla replied.

Five minutes later, Rob was slowing the rental car, already wheezing from ascending into the mountains, at an old gate across what had once been a drive. It looked like it had been a long time since the gate had opened. They had not seen any other structures of any kind for miles, not homes, barns, gates, or fences.

Rob pulled the rental car alongside the gate, stopped, and turned off the engine.

"I think this is it," Rob said as he pulled his cellphone from his pocket and gave it a swipe.

"Some friend," Marla said, smiling.

"Wait'll you see him," Rob said back quietly, his cellphone already ringing.

Minutes later, a small figure with a big beard and some sort of mountaineering clothes, looking to Marla more like a gnome than a man, appeared at the gate.

"Friends!" the man called.

"Good to see you!" Rob called back from the rental car's open window. He and Marla got out to greet the gnome-like figure.

Marla soon learned from their brief conversation at the old gate that Rob had long known the man whom Blake had then met in Las Vegas. They had stayed in touch since, Marla didn't know about what.

Within a couple of minutes of conversation, Rob had confirmed that he would return to pick up the man on Sunday morning to attend the championship race. Marla had no clue yet as to why, but she listened respectfully, especially insofar as she felt a strange instant liking for the man.

Rob and Marla departed shortly later, waving to the gnome-like figure as he retreated into the distance behind the still-closed and evidently long-closed gate.

"Are you going to fill me in?" Marla said with a wry smile as Rob turned the rental car around to let it begin its long, easy roll back down the mountain.

Rob spent the next few minutes trying to convince Marla of the value of the man's insights, for both Rob and Blake. Marla liked the man but had little interest in those insights. She was nonetheless glad for Rob and Blake that they had such a peculiar friend.

On the way back, as they gradually grew nearer to civilization, Marla pointed out something ahead of them on the highway. As they drew nearer, it looked like a disabled vehicle with its lights still on. As they drew up to the vehicle, they discovered that it was a pickup truck parked in the middle of the highway, headlights on, driver and passenger doors open, interior light on, and cabin empty. Just sitting there, in the middle of the road, in the dark night.

"Keep your eyes open, Honey," Rob said as they pulled up alongside the vehicle, "Could be a trap."

Rob needn't have said so. Marla shared Rob's military background. She was already on full alert.

Their eyes scanned the roadside, watching for potential assailants hiding in the ditches. They simultaneously studied the ditches and hillsides rising into the distance for signs of the truck's occupants, fighting, drunk, injured, or engaged in other private activities.

The bare desert provided no shelter from their view. In the moonlight, Rob and Marla could easily see into the distance up the grand hills in either direction, to the night skyline. Nothing. No sign of any driver or other occupant.

The pickup truck just sat there, motor running, lights on, doors open, in the middle of the highway.

Rob maneuvered the rental car slowly past the eerie truck. He let the rental car roll slowly on. With no one to rescue and nothing else obvious to do, Rob wasn't in the mood to stop. He turned to Marla.

"Want to stop?"

"Let's get out of here," Marla replied.

"Probably best," Rob agreed.

"New Mexico may be the Land of Enchantment," Marla quipped minutes later, still thinking of the eerie truck, "But Arizona will also do."

Rob nodded, smiling. Marla's humorous acknowledgment of the inexplicable event slowly dissipated its otherworldly chill.

Blake and Diana had a different kind of evening, on the opposite end of the social spectrum from taking a quiet drive to briefly meet a recluse. Blake's team owner had arranged a soiree of sorts. The owner had invited Blake and Diana.

The gathering wasn't at a reception hall or other public event space but instead at a very large and exclusive private residence. Diana never learned whose residence it was. She imagined that it belonged to the team owner's friend or business associate. The team owner seemed at ease and at home in the residence, as if he might visit frequently or perhaps even stay there during race weeks. But again, Diana couldn't tell.

Diana also couldn't discern the gathering's purpose or the profile of the invites. It wasn't even clearly a team event. None of the team owner's other drivers were present. Diana recognized only a handful of other guests as in some way connected with the team, among the dozens of invited guests. The event wasn't thanking team sponsors.

The evening seemed instead to just be a purely social event, one without purpose other than to gather mostly disconnected people together in the hopes that they might enjoy meeting and spending an evening with one another.

Diana realized early in the evening the magic and power of such mixed, purposeless, loosely planned events. She imagined the team owner considering the invitation list and thinking, *Oh, so-and-so might appreciate meeting so-and-so*, out of the owner's extraordinarily wide circle of acquaintances. But then, the owner might instead have just sat down to list an odd assortment of friends and acquaintances, thinking, *Let's see what magic the evening brings*.

It was also one of those gatherings that wasn't a cocktail party, wasn't a beer bash, wasn't a dinner, and wasn't a dance. Whoever helped the owner plan the event had the wisdom and skill to conceal the plan. The effect was to leave the guests with a grand riddle, asking them to consider again, out of a pleasant evening's happenstance, that most-important-of-all questions, *Why am I here?*

The vast and intriguing home's understated dignity, together with the event's parallel elegance, helped Blake, Diana, and the other guests answer that all-important question.

They were all *here* both at a specific time and place, at the residence in early November during stock-car championship week, and simultaneously in no specific time or place, at a residence whose owner they didn't know, at a time unrelated to any particular event, for a gathering that revealed no express purpose.

The gathering thus challenged its guests to give up thinking of their immediate purposes, *why am I here?*, the answer to which seemed to be *no immediate purpose*, to dwell for an evening in their eternal purpose, *why am*

I here?, the answer to which seemed to be to discover eternal divinity in oneself and in one another.

The vast home's understated dignity promoted that sense of momentarily giving up the immediate for the eternal, the profane for the divine. The home made Diana feel as if it was beckoning her to explore its beguiling spaces until she found the one its owner had composed specifically to please, satisfy, and comfort her. And then she was to linger there, in her room, until she could discern the composer's particular pleasure in having also created her.

The host's eccentric but delectable provisioning for the gathering had the same effect. Diana felt as if she was walking in Eden's garden, without any particular need for nutrients or hunger to quell, but nonetheless sampling the eclectic delicacies simply because they were there for her delight.

The enchanting gathering also made Diana feel as if the hidden host had arranged the guests just for Blake and her to meet. For Diana, the effect was a bit like the games people play of asking one another whom above all others they would most like to meet. Einstein, Edison, Curie, or Nehru? Augustine, Gandhi, Mandela, or Joan of Arc? Mozart, Gaga, Lennon, or Bernstein? Diana never had a good answer because she always felt like she would prefer above all to meet a room of pleasantly disposed strangers. At this gathering, she did.

Somewhere in the evening, Diana thought again of Blake's open-wheel driver friend and the driver's girlfriend, the two who, though not yet even engaged, had obviously complemented one another so well. As she and Blake moved slowly about the residence, meeting or renewing acquaintances with individuals and couples, Diana considered how she and Blake complemented one another.

Diana and Blake weren't relative opposites like the open-wheel driver and his girlfriend. Yes, Diana could see that Blake was routinely confident, while she was often not. Blake was naturally bold in action, while she was not. She, on the other hand, was generally quick with a word, while Blake was generally not. And she was naturally goal directed, single minded, while Blake was often not. But on the whole, she and Blake were much more alike, compatible, than balanced by opposing forces.

Their complementarianism was thus of a different sort. They didn't so much match by opposites, nor by similarities. They instead seemed to come together in a sort of congenial combustibility, like oxygen and fuel ready for the spark. As they moved about the residence, chatting with others, Diana sensed that they were more together than they were apart.

Fire needs both oxygen and fuel. A meal deserves both sweet and savory. A day needs both the afternoon warmth and the morning chill. Diana wasn't always one and Blake the other. Diana and Blake seemed instead to easily trade roles and personalities as they moved in and out of conversations that evening. But they were clearly much more and much better together than they were alone.

Blake drove Diana back toward her hotel on his way to the motorhome when they finally left the gathering. On the way, Diana soon broke their sated silence with a surprising suggestion.

"You and Marla could start a race team," Diana said.

Blake glanced over at Diana with a smile.

"You know, in a lower series, where you can hire and mentor younger drivers," Diana clarified.

Blake glanced over again with another smile.

"And let Marla run it so it doesn't burden you," Diana added.

Blake laughed. Diana stopped, sitting silently for a moment.

"I don't want you to lose her," Diana finally said.

Surprising herself, Diana almost burst into tears. Diana had thought that she and Blake might just have a brief, quiet conversation about the future. Instead, she had blurted out ideas as emotion rose within her. Diana suddenly worried what Blake might think. But Blake quickly eased her concern.

"We're not going to lose her," Blake replied in a gentle voice, adding, "And yes, we should be thinking and speaking of those things."

Blake reached over and placed a hand on Diana's forearm, saying, "And thank you for bringing it up. That took some courage."

Blake's kindness made Diana want to cry even more. It had been a perfect evening.

14

"Unloaded fast," the crew chief said to the race engineer beside him atop Blake's pit box.

Blake's car was circling the track around them. Lap after lap showed good speed, and they hadn't even made any significant adjustments yet.

"Ready to bring it in?" the crew chief radioed to Blake inside the car.

"What do you have in mind?" Blake's response came over the radio.

"Nothing, if it still feels good to you," the crew chief said.

"You guys nailed it," came Blake's response. He added, "Give me a few more laps to see if it changes."

But Blake wasn't looking for changes in the car. He wasn't concerned about a fall-off in the car's long-run speed. He was instead thinking of his open-wheel friend's sight line and awareness discussion.

Phoenix Speedway has a track configuration like no other. Every track is unique, even the mile-and-a-half ovals that seem to try to replicate one another. They don't. Each track has at least slightly different curves, banking, pit road entries and exits, track surface age, and certainly different sight lines along the fences and horizon.

But Phoenix Speedway is more different than the rest. Its one-mile trioval configuration nearly makes it like a road course laid atop an oval.

At one end, through turns one and two, the track has a traditional wide-sweeping curve, one end of the oval. But that big curve has spare banking, just eight or nine degrees. The cars have the look and feel of sweeping around an ice rink's end, trying to maintain tiny bits of grip so as not to shoot up the extra-wide track into the tire-debris pebbles.

The track's other end, though, is the real anomaly. Turn three begins what might have been another big, wide-sweeping curve of a traditional oval. That curve has slightly greater banking than the curve at the track's other end, more like ten to eleven degrees. But instead of completing another big sweeping curve into a straightaway for a traditional oval, that second curve straightens out about two thirds of the way around into a short chute.

The start/finish line is in the middle of the short chute.

The short chute is just long enough to jut the track's other straightaway out so that it isn't parallel with the other straightaway. The short chute then ends with the rest of the bend necessary to make the straightaway connect with the other end's sweeping curve.

The layout is hard to describe, harder to learn how to race consistently.

Complicating the track's peculiar layout is the track's wide racing surface without clearly delineated lines. Anywhere on the track, a driver could move up or down to find a faster line. The only thing stopping a driver from making a new line is the infield wall, well down away from the racing surface except at one end of the track, and the outside fence.

Coming out of the short chute, drivers court that outside fence, kissing it regretfully.

But Phoenix Speedway injects still other anomalies. Drivers may attempt a shortcut across the curve out of the short chute, which is also where cars enter the track off pit road. Taking the shortcut, though, requires the car to come down off the banking and onto an apron, skipping the car across the apron.

Desperate cars will try the shortcut. But at various points in the race, many cars may try to do so, finding it to be not so desperate. The shortcut sometimes works but other times doesn't. If one car proves it to work, other cars will quickly join in the fun. It's an extraordinary feature for a racetrack.

Just as peculiar as the track layout itself is the great grandstand looming around, and nearly over, turns three and four including all of the short chute. The grandstand, with its skyboxes atop, follows the peculiar layout of the racing surface below it. It looks like a broken boomerang. The looming grandstand also soon begins to shade that end of the racetrack. Drivers seem to dive out of the bright desert sun and into a cave, especially toward dusk.

Perhaps the most-peculiar feature of Phoenix Speedway, though, lies just beyond the track and grandstand. The track's founders sited it in the desert hills, indeed in the Estrella Mountains.

One hill, known as *Monument Hill*, lies so close to the track that it's a popular place for viewing. Monument Hill, though, doesn't commemorate fallen soldiers or other ancestors. Instead, atop Monument Hill is a United States Geological Survey bench marker surveyors used to lay out all of Arizona. Those straight lines you see on a map marking the state's borders? They originate from Phoenix Speedway.

Racers, of course, aren't thinking of geology or history when navigating the extraordinary track. But their eyesight and nervous systems may be subtly accounting for hints of the track's bumps, curves, and best racing lines, from Monument Hill and other hills, mountains, and features surrounding the track.

Blake thus wanted to run more practice laps to see what his increased awareness within the car and out to the horizon might pick up in slight speed improvements, just as he had picked up fractions of speed at Martinsville. It was worth a try.

"Ready to bring it in?" the crew chief asked Blake over the radio after a few more laps.

"No," Blake radioed back, "A few more laps."

Blake had already run way more practice laps than any other car, especially in that Blake hadn't left the track for his crew to make car adjustments.

"Just about done now?" the crew chief radioed Blake after a few more laps.

One slip at the wheel, and Blake could skid the car up the track into the wall, bringing out the backup car and potentially crushing the team's championship hopes.

"Soon," Blake replied.

Blake was not trying to find speed. Blake was trying not to think at all but instead to see, hear, and feel absolutely everything going on inside and outside his car. *Just see, hear, and feel*, he kept thinking, not thinking. *Let your senses find the speed*, he kept thinking, not thinking.

Finally, the crew chief saw Blake's car slow, then pull down onto the apron and down pit road. Blake remained silent in the car, still trying not to think but to let his senses and nervous system somehow process what he had just experienced on the track.

The crew chief looked at the race engineer next to him and shrugged. The race engineer shrugged back. The crew chief raised a forefinger to his temple and made a circling motion, as if to say, *He's crazy, isn't he?* They both smiled and then chuckled. But they both also suspected that yet again, Blake was onto something. He had consistently run the fastest practice times, and those times had consistently gotten better.

The crew chief and race engineer knew that they were working with a gifted driver. Yet they were only just learning that they might be working with a genius, generational talent.

The crew chief had entered his professional relationship with Blake as the veteran. From the start, he had conceived of his role as bringing along yet another highly skilled but not yet fully mature driver. Their partnership had been fruitful from the start. The crew chief's veteran wisdom had seemed just the thing to speed this next skilled driver's rise.

Yet across the course of their relationship, the crew chief had begun to feel that their roles had flipped, that

Blake was more and more the veteran and the crew chief more and more the student. The crew chief might not have thought that flip to be unusual, if it had occurred over the course of a decade or two. But it had instead occurred over the course of just a year or two.

Blake's car rolled through the pit road gate and back to the garage. The crew chief, race engineer, and pit crew followed.

As he walked back to the garage to meet Blake following the long practice run, the crew chief thought for the first time that he may never have been the veteran crew chief to the student Blake. He instead began to think that Blake had always been the prodigy genius, indulging the crew chief as a necessary adjunct. Time would tell, the crew chief thought. But a championship win this week would tell a lot.

Blake's crew did little to the car in the way of adjustments following practice. They instead did the routine things crews do to trim the car for qualifying. Qualifying would be the next afternoon, Saturday, the day before the championship race.

By championship weekend, the air buzzed with excitement. Blake, Diana, Rob, and Marla tried to keep to a usual schedule. Championship weekend of course brought extra visits from sponsor representatives, dignitaries, and celebrities.

Marla, especially, was busy fielding calls and requests for Blake's time. Diana stayed at Marla's elbow, helping where she could. Both tried to be judicious in protecting Blake's time while also generous in arranging access. It was a fine balance to maintain.

Blake, though, seemed fully up to the task. Diana marveled at how Blake moved through Friday and Saturday, appearing to do so without any of the jitteriness that she felt. Even Marla showed hints of the same overly excited energy, the kind that can quickly exhaust one. Blake? None of it. Cool as a cucumber.

A lot rode, though, on qualifying, which started late Saturday afternoon.

Qualifying position means more at Phoenix Speedway than at some other tracks. Despite the track's anomalous layout with a wide racing surface and little banking, or perhaps because of those features, passing can be especially difficult. A slower car can certainly make it difficult for a faster car to work its way past. Falling well back in the field can be fatal to a successful outcome. Racing from the back to the front, or even the middle to the front, is a rare feat.

The four championship racers would be the last to qualify. They would have the full advantage of letting the other cars develop and refine the groove.

Diana was with Marla in the corporate suites, greeting sponsor representatives. Unlike at many other race events, championship qualifying was a well-attended event. The corporate suites weren't jammed, but they were full. Marla appreciated Diana's help moving swiftly back and forth among the suites, greeting guests, helping guests with logistics, and responding to requests.

Rob was his usual invisible self, monitoring security across the track and grounds, keeping his steady hand on the pulse of the grand weekend's events.

Blake was in his car early, well before the necessary time to join the cars in the qualifying queue. He wanted to sit quietly in the car, letting his senses attune themselves to the car's interior. He wanted his mind to grow still so that his whole being could absorb the sense of the car around him, as an extension of his person.

Many who engage with commitment to their trades and professions develop an affinity for their tools and equipment. Some come to treat those artificial things as extensions of their person. The premier surgeon doesn't wield a scalpel as a scalpel but as the surgeon's own innate ability to sever tissue. The surgeon operating arthroscopically, peering into the video monitor of a tiny remote camera at the end of a cable inserted into the patient's cavity while manipulating triggers to control remote tools, must lose the sense of those mediating tools so as to feel as if touching the internal tissues directly.

Likewise, excavators begin to feel as if the many-ton hoe simply extends their arm and hand deep below the ground to move the soil and stones. Long-haul drivers can feel their rig's tires on the wet, freezing, and slippery pavement as if the tires were their own feet. Lawyers manipulate their keyboards executing electronic research as if walking through libraries lifting books and turning pages. And graphic designers move their pixels about the screen as if lying on their backs on a scaffold painting the ceiling of the Sistine Chapel with a physical brush in their own hands.

That's how it was for Blake, sitting quietly in his race car, contemplating qualifying for the championship race. His head didn't swim with scenarios. His heart didn't pound with fear, fright, and stress. The steering wheel didn't feel like a foreign object, and his seat didn't feel like a tomb.

Instead, the car faded from the impressions Blake's senses suggested to his frontal cortex, until the car breathed and pulsed as if his unthinking autonomic nervous system regulated it right along with his heart rate, blood pressure, and respiration.

"You're up, Bud," the crew chief radioed Blake from atop the pit box.

A pit crew member motioned to Blake to head the car from the garage lane onto pit road, in the short remaining qualifying queue.

At another track and at another time, the crew chief might have had some last-minute advice for Blake based on what other qualifying runs had shown. But Phoenix Speedway's bewildering layout left little opportunity for a single sound tweak here or there. The variables and options were too many for the crew chief to give any sound advice.

But the crew chief also sensed that advice would have distracted Blake from something better that he was discovering. The crew chief's instructions were thus unusually sparse.

"One more to go, then you," the crew chief radioed, although the queue ahead of Blake made his turn obvious.

"Your track," the crew chief radioed as the car ahead of Blake flew past the pit road exit and on around the track toward the end of the qualifying run.

Blake didn't know who was leading qualifying or what the qualifying times were showing. He could easily have found out if he had wanted to do so, from his crew chief directly or from the pit road reactions and other clues. But he instead kept his focus on sensing the car and the sight lines and stimuli around him.

Blake brought his car down pit road and out its exit onto the track. With his tires warmed and engine fluids coursing, he accelerated smoothly down the backstretch, around turns one and two, up the frontstretch, and around the grandstand curve into the short chute across the starting line to begin his qualifying run.

Blake later had no recollection to report to his crew chief, team owner, or the media of how his qualifying run had felt. Blake didn't feel his car through the qualifying run. He couldn't say that the car was tight or loose on entry or exit, responsive or lagging in throttle, or easy or hard on braking.

Instead, Blake's qualifying run just happened, without Blake's thought. He didn't recall noting any challenge or opportunity during the run, or any stimulus to which he had adjusted. It was as if he was an eagle taking flight, when eagles have no need for thinking how to fly, or as if he was a cheetah running down its prey, when cheetahs have no need for thinking how to run.

One championship driver had qualified before Blake. Two championship drivers qualified after Blake. Blake bested all three and the rest of the field. The pole position for the championship race was his. He would begin the race as the clear championship favorite.

15

Blake's pole win brought a crush of attention. Attention would have been intense without a pole win. The pole win simply brought it to a fever or frenzy.

Blake, though, only bore some of that burden of media, public, racing community, and team attention. Marla and Diana bore the brunt of it.

Blake's pole win meant Marla had more media appearances and sponsor contacts to coordinate, more demands to which she needed to show that Blake had quickly and appropriately responded. Diana helped.

Quotes from Blake embedded in replies to texts and emails satisfied many of the demands. Brief appearances, if possible stacked one atop another, satisfied most of the rest. By late Saturday, the flurry had exhausted Marla and Diana. They both hoped not Blake.

Rob was up early on Sunday morning. He had a certain friend up in the mountains to pick up, to bring to the race track for the championship race. But Rob had arranged to make the trip earlier than strictly necessary. He had a growing sense that more was at hand than just helping a friend watch an exciting race.

Rob's rental car wheezed its way up the mountain. The yurt man was standing at his gate, as Rob wheeled the tired rental car in a U-turn on the road to pull it up at the gate, ready to head back downhill.

"Good morning!" Rob greeted his friend as the friend opened the passenger door to hop in.

The yurt man nodded shyly, shrugged, and mumbled, "Good morning," already feeling awkward about an escort to a stock-car-racing championship, of all things.

"Going to be a fun day," Rob said casually in an effort to put his friend more at ease.

"Yes?" the yurt man replied with a quizzical look, "Is that why you race, for fun?"

Rob instantly remembered that the yurt man didn't make small talk. Isolation will do that to you. Every word carries weight.

"You know, you're right," Rob admitted, "Fun probably wasn't the right word."

Rob thought for a moment before saying with a smile, "An *interesting* day, how about that?"

"Yes," the yurt man replied seriously, "I'd say so."

They were mostly silent the rest of the way down the mountain.

"Let me show you some viewing options," Rob offered his friend when they reached the track's parking lots.

"Okay," the yurt man said in a simple reply.

Rob led his friend from the parking lot up to the skyboxes. It was early enough that they met virtually no one along the way.

"Quite a view, huh?" Rob said as they looked from one of the skyboxes down across the track and up into the mountains.

"Yes," the yurt man nodded in another simple reply. He hadn't looked impressed. Rob realized that his friend saw views like this one every day.

Rob led his friend from the skyboxes under the track and to the infield, where he pointed out some spots from which his friend might watch the race.

"They'd be loud but exciting, right in the thick of things," Rob offered.

"Yes," the yurt man said in the same simple reply.

Rob tried to read his friend. Then, he thought of one more place.

"Come on, I've got an idea," Rob said, turning back toward the tunnel under the track.

Within a few minutes, they had made their way well up above the track to some roughly outlined seating areas in the desert on the side of Monument Hill. The track below seemed a safe distance away.

Rob turned, looked back down toward the track, and made a grand motion, as if to offer the seating and view to his friend. This time, though, he made no assessment.

"Ah, perfect," the yurt man said, adding, "I'd be very comfortable here. Thank you."

Rob smiled, almost laughed.

"Well, we've got quite a while before race-day festivities begin," Rob said, offering, "I'd be happy if you would accompany me on some light duties."

The yurt man nodded. Rob figured that his friend's nod was the equivalent of glad assent. They descended the hill together.

Rob led his friend toward Blake's motorhome. Looking at his watch, Rob calculated that Diana and Marla should be there by now. Rob hoped to make his usual Sunday-morning stop to see Blake, before Rob headed off on security duties.

Diana and Marla had made their way to Blake's motorhome earlier than usual. They agreed that they wanted to soak up every minute of the championship day. They found Blake in his usual good spirits. And no one wanted to rush the day. The day would require extraordinary energy from each of them. The morning wasn't the time to expend reserves.

Knowing their need, the three spent some quiet time reminiscing rather than speculating on the coming day. Soon, though, came Rob's light knock on the motorhome door.

Marla opened the motorhome's door to see Rob and the yurt man. Rob smiled up at Marla. The yurt man looked impassively away.

"We have a visitor," Marla said politely, turning to Blake and Diana.

Blake shrugged nonchalantly. Diana raised her eyebrows.

"I believe someone you've met before," Marla said, this time only to Blake.

Blake raised his eyebrows. Then, a thought dawned, and a smile spread across Blake's face.

"Invite him in," Blake said in a pleasant voice to Marla.

Marla did so. Diana watched as Rob entered followed by a gnome-ish looking man of thick frame and with a long, full beard. He looked to Diana, as he had looked to Blake and Marla on their prior introductions, as if he was wearing some form of old mountain or woods garb.

Diana rose, offered her hand, and said good to meet you.

"Yes," the man replied, looking at Diana's hand as if not knowing what to do.

Diana withdrew her hand, slowly so as not to embarrass the man.

"Ready to take a walk, Honey?" Marla asked Diana with a smile, giving a slight tip of her head toward the curious figure.

Diana nodded. The two left. As soon as they did, Marla tried to explain the man's significance. Like Marla had been before her, Diana was unconcerned and not especially interested.

"Boys will be boys, eh?" Marla quipped.

Diana smiled and shrugged.

Back in the motorhome, Rob had already taken his usual seat while offering a seat to his friend. The yurt man perched uncomfortably on the edge of the seat rather than settling back into it, as the seat clearly invited.

Blake had already risen to welcome his friend, although Blake had wisely not bothered to offer a handshake. Blake had gauged from their earlier meeting and Diana's just-frustrated attempt that handshakes were not among the yurt man's few social habits.

Blake hadn't expected his friend's appearance. Rob would ordinarily have told Blake of Rob's plans. But Rob hadn't known how the yurt man might respond to any of Rob's offers and actions that day. Rob had half expected his friend not even to be at his gate at the appointed hour that morning. And so Rob had not burdened Blake with the uncertain possibility of their friend's motorhome visit.

But although Blake hadn't expected their friend's appearance, Blake nonetheless welcomed it. Indeed, more than welcoming it, Blake suspected that some act of providence was right then preparing to unfold through the visit.

Blake, though, didn't have any idea how to prompt that providence. Providence follows its own course in any case, impermeable to human prompting, rather being the tool of the divine.

And so Blake's first few words were only to tell his friend, *Thank you*, and that, *Your messages have been meaningful and helpful.*

The yurt man had simply nodded in acknowledgment of Blake's gratitude. He hadn't replied, *You're welcome*, or, *Oh, I'm so glad*, as others more accustomed to social graces might have replied. But Blake hadn't expected his friend to do so. Indeed, his friend's doing so would have disappointed Blake.

Blake was already well attuned to his friend's preferences. Blake, for instance, intended to speak as sparingly and precisely as he possibly could, if Blake spoke at all. And Blake was exactly right in doing so. Blake didn't know the yurt man's history, but he had once been a coder, where every symbol must have its precise place for the code to work.

Rob, Blake, and their friend sat in silence for a moment, attuning to one another's presence. Surprisingly, the yurt man was the first to speak.

"What is a championship?" he asked.

Blake replied with little hesitation, describing it as a *superordinate construct* nearer the top of a *peculiar social activity*.

"I agree," the yurt man said after a moment's consideration.

They sat in silence again for a minute before the yurt man spoke again.

"Does one pursue a championship, then?" he asked.

Blake nodded, explaining simply that *superordinate constructs invite pursuit*.

"I agree," the yurt man said again after another moment's consideration.

Soon, the yurt man had another question, asking, "How do you know it's a proper superordinate construct to pursue?"

Blake replied, again with little hesitation, saying simply that *one properly pursues superordinate constructs that point to the highest entity*.

"I agree," the yurt man said yet again, this time without the need for consideration.

"How do you recognize the highest entity?" the yurt man next asked, this time without pause to formulate the question.

Blake promptly replied *as the creator of all constructs out of material that the creator orders into meaning.*

The yurt man no longer found cause to affirm each of Blake's answers. Instead, the yurt man continued tumbling out question after question, to each of which Blake stated a direct and precise answer with which the yurt man evidently agreed, given his willingness to prose the next corollary question.

"How do you best pursue a championship?" the yurt man asked.

By *attending to things in their priority within their hierarchical order*, Blake replied.

"How do you recognize their priority?" the yurt man asked.

By *whether they point to higher or lower-order constructs*, Blake replied.

"And what does it mean to attend?" the yurt man asked.

To *focus awareness, particularly of the senses, on those things*, Blake replied.

"And how should one treat disorder?" the yurt man asked.

As *a remainder out of which to tap potential rather than an enemy to tyrannize*, Blake replied.

On their inquiry went, addressing time, space, meaning, material, customs, chaos, and related subjects.

Rob watched and listened, while monitoring his time and Blake's time.

"Well," the yurt man finally concluded, "That was refreshing. I've thought about these things for a long time. I have much more to consider. Do you have any questions for me?"

"Just one," Blake replied promptly, "What does winning a championship bring?"

The yurt man blinked, as if looking into the future. Soon, he spoke.

"It depends on how you win it," the yurt man replied, adding, "Ask me again after the race."

Blake and Rob both smiled. For the first time, the yurt man smiled, too.

"Say, that's right," Rob observed as he stood up. He added, addressing Blake, "Our friend has agreed to meet your team owner after the race, which he's going to watch from Monument Hill."

Blake looked at his friend with a special smile. The yurt man looked back, sharing Blake's smile.

"Fitting, isn't it," Blake observed to his friend, "That you would watch a championship race from atop a hill that centered and measured the land far beyond what the eye can see."

"Yes," the yurt man smiled back at Blake, "The championship's conceptual axis meeting the land's material axis gathered in the heart of the champion who raced."

"Interesting," Blake replied.

The yurt man nodded and turned to go. Rob opened the motorhome's door. Rob and Blake watched the yurt man leave. As he disappeared from view, Rob was the first to speak.

"Now that was an eternal moment," he said.

"Yes," Blake replied, adding with a sly smile, "Interesting indeed."

Pre-race festivities followed their familiar order. It was the last race of the long season, the championship race. But just because it was the season's final, championship race is no reason to abandon ritual order.

Driver introductions preceded a trackside prayer and the national anthem, ending with an awe-striking military flyover, which the great pack of race cars would soon top in their rush across the starting line. Drivers gave their last kiss to their wife or girlfriend and hugs to any trackside children.

Displaying everything from relaxed good humor to grim tension, they then shoehorned themselves through their car windows and into their driver's seats to don helmets and gloves. Crew chiefs ensured that window netting was properly fixed in place.

And then the race's grand marshal gave the great command, the last one of the calendar year and racing season, *Driver's, start your engines!*

Diana and Blake had agreed that Diana would watch the race not from her usual spot atop Blake's pit box but instead while helping Marla high above the track in the corporate suites. It hadn't been a hard choice. Diana wasn't sure she could handle a championship race atop the pit box. And Marla would appreciate the help, while Diana learned more about her coming role next year.

Billy the spotter was atop the grandstands, binoculars in hand. The crew chief and race engineer had their headsets on atop the pit box. The team owner wandered up and down from one of his team's pit boxes to another, encouraging each of his pit crews to have the best possible race.

Rob stopped by the corporate suites to watch the race's start with Marla and Diana. The yurt man stood near the summit of Monument Hill, watching the race cars emerge from pit road to begin circling the track, as if stalking invisible prey just ahead.

Other friends and acquaintances of Blake and Diana were present and in place for the race's start, too. Diana's college roommate Julie, who had played a big role in Diana's introduction to stock-car racing and Blake, had flown in from Denton Beach at Diana's invitation, to watch the race from the corporate suites.

Munn and his family, whom Blake, Diana, Rob, and Marla had befriended barely two months earlier on a track security case, had driven out to watch the championship race. They were right at that moment meeting the yurt man, from their own vantage point on Monument Hill.

Fred, the psychologist race official who a half-year earlier had helped Blake retrieve the wedding ring he had purchased to propose to Diana, was patrolling the pit boxes up and down pit road, to ensure his pit-inspector officials were all in place.

Fred's centenarian friend Lightnin', the Denton International Speedway ticket taker who had saved Diana from the clutches of a Russian double agent and helped foil that agent's later designs on the life of Blake, was at her television set at home, watching the race's start. Lightnin' would be the first to greet them all for the Denton 500, the next season's first points race in just a few short months.

One other figure was also present, one whose attendance no one other than Blake himself would discover or would have foreseen. High in the grandstand, out of everyone's way, and keeping to himself, sat Blake and Marla's father, in a seat the ticket for which Blake had sent him, as a last fitting act of perfect alignment. Blake was finally and fully ready for the championship race to start.

16

"No need to fight him," the crew chief radioed Blake immediately after the green flag had flown, the race pack had gotten up to speed, and the cars had flown out of turn two and down the backstretch toward the wide curve of turns three and four.

The second-place car on Blake's outside, also a championship contender, was side drafting and pinching Blake's car down low for entry into turn one. The crew chief was signaling to let the other driver take the lead.

Blake promptly did so, dropping back to second and then, under a similar charge from the third-place car, also a championship contender, back to third around turns one and two. Blake's fans in the great crowd groaned, while the fans of the other two championship contenders who had just passed Blake cheered.

Race fans, though, wouldn't necessarily have known that Blake preferred third place over first place right at that moment in the race.

Blake and his crew chief had discerned at least one championship-race strategy, drawn from their approach of monitoring and responding to the other championship drivers' strategies. That strategy was that because leading the race made it hard to respond to the other drivers' strategies, they shouldn't sacrifice other advantages to lead the race.

Better, they discerned, to *lead from behind* than in front, although racers, like soldiers, aren't generally familiar with the construct of *leading from behind*. One leads from in front, except perhaps in this one championship race.

What Blake and his crew chief discerned is that the race leader generally has several advantages including things like clean air, choice of racing lines, and first one down pit road and into the pit box on a yellow caution.

But, they also knew, the race leader always has one disadvantage. The followers can see what the race leader does and can thus plot a more-advantageous strategy.

If, for instance, the race leader declines to pit for fresh tires, anyone behind the race leader can choose to have fresher tires than the leader, simply by pitting. If, on the other hand, the race leader decides to pit for fresh tires, anyone behind the leader can decline to pit in order to gain track position over the leader.

The same goes with taking two tires or four tires on a pit stop. If the leader takes four, many behind the leader can take two tires if they wish, with a better chance of beating the leader off pit road. If, on the other hand, the leader takes just two tires, many behind the leader can take four tires, for better grip than the leader when the race restarts.

Blake and his crew chief thus began the race with an eye toward finding that most-advantageous track position where they could best monitor and respond to their championship competitors.

With the race engineer's help running simulation after simulation back at the race facility, Blake and his crew chief learned that depending on where their championship competitors were, Blake's best place from which to control the race might be second place, fifth place, or even tenth or twelfth place, although likely no further back.

The race engineer, working with the simulator's analyst, had developed a shorthand computer program for the championship race, to help the race engineer tell Blake and the crew chief the best track position from which to control the race. The program took the other championship drivers' track positions and other variables, to predict Blake's best place at any point during the race.

As the two other championship contenders pulled ahead of Blake, the race engineer nodded to the crew chief, holding up three fingers.

"Let 'em go," the crew chief radioed Blake, "We're where we want to be in third."

Blake settled in for the long championship race. Each time a car tested Blake to pass, Billy would confirm the car's identity, the crew chief would look to the race engineer, and the race engineer would share any guidance on how hard Blake ought to race the challenging car, depending on where Blake should remain to respond best to the strategies of the other three championship contenders.

Blake thus fell back to fourth and then to fifth in the first stage, while saving his tires and protecting his car, without any cause for alarm. Indeed, when both championship contenders ahead of him also gave way to non-contender cars, falling back several positions, the race engineer calculated that Blake could relinquish additional positions if helpful to save his car.

Blake ran in seventh or eighth position for the rest of the first stage, just behind two of the championship contenders. When the green-checkered flag flew at the end of the stage, the three leading championship contenders were all between fifth and eighth place, with the other contender still well back in the pack.

In the corporate suites, Diana and Marla were unaware of Blake's unusual strategy. They assumed, like many fans and a few commentators, that Blake might be struggling with his car.

The opposite, though, was true: Blake was not only fully satisfied with his car but had also been saving its suspension, brakes, engine, tires, and body from wear, tear, bumps, and bruises. Blake felt as poised for the coming championship finish as he possibly could have been.

The first-stage caution, though, had given the trailing championship contender the advantage of responding to the strategies of the three contenders ahead of him. He had pitted before the stage-end caution. He thus had no need to pit with the other championship contenders on the stage-end caution. When the field assembled for the restart, the trailing contender was now the leading contender, with only slightly older tires.

The trailing contender had thus done what Blake had strategized to do, which was to trump the other contenders' strategies. Yet he had done so only at the end of the first stage. The race was far from over.

Blake now trailed all three championship contenders. But Blake trailed all three championship contenders by only a handful of track positions. And the race engineer would have put Blake in exactly that position, to best implement their monitor-and - respond strategy.

Race fans and commentators decried Blake's fall back behind all three other championship contenders. But Blake and his crew chief were in exactly the position they would have wished for at this point in the race. Other drivers might have unwisely pressed the issue. Instead, Blake further relaxed, growing even more in tune and aware of his car and the many other stimuli around him.

Race fans know that having all four championship contenders bunched near the front for much of the championship race is not that unusual. Championship contenders routinely run strong in the championship race. Indeed, championship contenders win the championship race outright far more often than chance alone would suggest.

The championship contenders generally being the best cars in the large field on championship Sunday makes sense. The teams preparing those cars are the teams that have best managed to navigate the innumerable challenges, obstacles, and anomalies of a long regular season followed by a three-round playoff. And the drivers behind the wheels of those cars have proven themselves the most consistent, and repeated times the best, of the field's drivers.

The success of the championship contenders on championship Sunday, against the ten-times-larger field of race cars, also proves just how elusive stock-car racing success is. The dozens of other drivers in the field, who are not championship contenders, are trying to win the championship race every bit as hard as the four championship contenders. A win by a non-contender in the championship race could bring all kinds of rewards and accolades, more so than just about any other single race.

But race wins aren't solely or even largely the product of *wanting* to win. Race wins are instead the product of so many variables and intangibles as to make victory seem more like a gift from above than a labor from below. And perhaps it always is.

Blake's broad and deep effort to set everything aright as he approached the championship race, from hopes and dreams to broken or ignored old relationships, had the character of a person who knows of his imminent death. But it also had the character of a person who knows of his immanent life. And it had the character of a person who knows that winning a championship just might be more a product of divine influence and grace than of mighty striving below.

The championship race's second stage unfolded very like the first stage. The three championship contenders ahead of Blake surged ahead, staying among the race leaders, while Blake lurked a couple or handful of cars behind those contenders.

The first real test of Blake's monitor-and-respond strategy came near the middle of the second stage. Non-contender cars began to pit early for fresh tires and gas. Those cars did so to get on a pit stop cycle that would let them race through stage two's end, pit fairly early in the third stage, and potentially make it to the race end without pitting again.

The three championship contenders ahead of Blake had a decision to make: either gamble with the pitting drivers or play it safe on the customary pit schedule. All three played it safe, staying on track, expecting to pit at stage two's end.

Blake and his crew chief now had the perfect opening to implement their monitor-and-respond strategy.

Indeed, the crew chief and engineer detected an opportunity to improve on the non-contending cars' pit-early strategy. Blake didn't have to beat those cars. He only had to beat the three championship contenders ahead of him. So the crew chief and engineer held Blake out on track for several more laps.

As they did so, they eliminated the risk that Blake would run out of gas at race end. They also ensured that Blake would have fresher tires at race end than the worn tires of those non-contending cars that had pitted early, and tires closer in wear to the tires that the three contenders would have when pitting even later.

At just the right moment, Blake's crew chief called Blake onto pit road. The crowd and commentators gasped. Diana and Marla gasped with them, up in the corporate suites. Blake was already behind the three championship contenders. Now, he would trail far behind them, but for some unforeseen fortuity, unable to catch them.

Speculation abounded that Blake's car was performing poorly or even disabled. The opposite, though, was true: Blake perceived the car to be sublime in its performance, like no car he had ever raced.

Blake's pit crew executed the perfect stop. Blake was back on track in the minimum possible time, on fresh tires and with a full tank of gas. But he was also out of touch with the leaders, including the three other championship contenders.

The race proceeded as if Blake had no chance, when the opposite was true: Blake controlled the race.

To the end of stage two, Blake kept his focus on the inside of his car and the stimuli he perceived around it. He blocked out all thoughts of the other championship contenders. He just sensed his car's performance, letting his awareness improve his lap times by the smallest margins that would prove crucial at the end of the long race.

Stage two ended with the three championship contenders near the front and Blake nearer the back. The three championship contenders pitted. Blake did not.

Blake's staying out gained him his lost track position. He was among the race leaders when the pack assembled for the restart. But every commentator and many race fans predicted correctly that he would quickly fall back on his old tires. Poor Blake, many thought.

Yet the wiser commentators and race fans could now see for the first time, or if they had sensed it earlier now see more clearly, that Blake had one fewer pit stops to make. Although he quickly fell back behind the other three championship contenders, Blake still controlled the race.

Moreover, depending on how the rest of the race unfolded, the other three championship contenders could no longer do anything about it. Blake's non-strategy approach had sealed their losing fate.

Aware that Blake was once again falling back in the pack behind the other three championship contenders, Diana and Marla tried their best to focus on their public relations duties at hand, up in the corporate suites.

The sponsor representatives and other dignitaries and guests in the corporate suites were generally also watching the race. A few were also watching broadcasts from within the suites.

Most of the guests in the suites rued Blake's fading track position, even consoling Marla and Diana. But hearing such concern, one of the sponsor representatives motioned to Marla and Diana over to a suite's corner. Pointing to the television monitor, the representative explained that the race commentators were beginning to say that Blake controlled the race.

The sponsor representative looked straight at Diana, then straight at Marla, a smile spreading across the representative's face. Diana and Marla looked at one another, processing what the representative had just shared. By the time they looked back at the representative, the representative was holding a hand up for a high five. His other hand held a can of beer.

Marla and Diana gave the representative his requested high five. Huge smiles of relief spread across their faces. Diana clutched her hands to her mouth, her eyes wide with excitement for the first time in the long race.

Rob had been catching bits of the race as he moved about the facility, checking on security, keeping his eyes open for developing issues, and trying to judge the pulse of the place. As often happened in championship races, the whole place, people and structures included, seemed to lean toward the drama on the track.

A terrorist might have judged it the most opportune time to trigger a spectacle distraction. But the sheer force of the championship endeavor seemed to strip evil of any possibility of such a distraction. Some things are just too weighty for evil to penetrate.

Rob thus gave more of his attention to the progress of the race. He had been aware of Blake's up and down standing. But Rob had also kept an ear open for more discerning judgments, as to whether Blake was winning or losing. And Rob had heard of the commentators' insight that Blake appeared now to control the race.

Rob decided to head for the corporate suites to join Marla and Diana for the race's finish.

High in the grandstand, sitting in a seat his championship-contender son had only at the last minute sent him, an older man had also watched the race unfold. That man understood racing. Racing had been in his family and in his blood. He had passed that racing blood on to his championship-contender son, even though he had not passed along much else of good.

17

"Coming to pit road," the crew chief radioed Blake, "Pit road this lap."

Blake expertly steered the car low on turns one and two, slowing the car to pit-road speed at the last instant, and bringing it down pit road to his stall. The pit crew flew into motion. In no time, Blake's car had four fresh tires and a full tank of gas, with no adjustments. Blake was back on track in the minimum time, although now well back in the pack again.

Blake had no more pit stops to make. He had plenty of gas to make it to the end, even well beyond to cover any restarts that might extend the race.

Other cars had already pitted a dozen or more laps earlier, right at the outer edge for enough gas to make it to the race's end. With fresh tires for a dozen laps before Blake pitted, those cars were now ahead of Blake as he merged back into traffic from his pit stop. But those cars were not championship contenders.

The three other championship contenders were well out in front. But they all had to make one more stop. None had enough gas to reach the finish. They all would need fresh tires, too.

The three other championship contenders still had strategies to deploy. They could still gain an advantage over one another. They could pit early. They could take two tires rather than four. They could read and react to one another's strategies for that advantage.

But the three championship contenders could no longer affect Blake. Nothing they did would regain the advantage Blake had gained over them much earlier in the race when getting on a pit-stop schedule that eliminated his last extra pit stop. And the three championship contenders were likewise at the mercy of the many non-contending cars that had also already made their last pit stop. The three other contenders were trapped.

The only hope the three other championship contenders had was for late-race cautions to bunch the field often enough for the contenders to work their way up to Blake's bumper, where they would have fresher tires and a good shot of beating him to the checkered flag.

Blake still trailed much of the field and was way back of the three other championship contenders, with the race near its end. An uninformed fan watching the race would have concluded that Blake had surely lost the championship.

But the race commentators were now listing the many cars that could make it to the end on gas, including Blake. And they were pointing out that Blake would be ahead of the three other championship contenders as soon as those three made their last pit stop. The realization had dawned across the grandstand and grounds, and across the world watching on television or listening on radio, that Blake was now the championship favorite.

New motor racing fans sometimes express frustration at not knowing who is actually winning the race. To new motor racing fans, the car running out front is the apparent winner, especially if the lead is big and the end of the race nearing. That's how it is with track and field, and horse racing. What your eyes show you is the truth.

But that's not motor racing, where informed fans may know full well that the leader has certainly lost.

Pit stops are the reason. Cars can't, like horses and humans, just run a little longer by trying a little harder. Cars run out of gas. And when they run out of gas, they stop. Dead on the track.

Indeed, stock-car racing has a history, wonderful or notorious depending on who is your favorite racing legend, of cars losing the race on the last lap by running out of gas, when their pit-stop-strategy gamble lost.

The three championship contenders ahead of Blake weren't going to run out of gas. They were going to make the necessary pit stop. But the necessity of that pit stop meant that even though they were now *leading* the race, they were not *winning* the race. They had instead already lost.

Stock-car races thus typically involve a frequent shuffling and reshuffling of racing positions throughout the race.

The races where every leading car pits with other leading cars so that the lead never significantly reshuffles are rare. Relatively few races involve a leader taking control of the race early and staying out front for the entire race. And when that happens, many race fans complain, especially if the winner was not their favorite driver.

The stock-car racing association could easily eliminate the shuffling and reshuffling dynamic. The rules could make all cars pit together. Or the rules could make stages short enough or the gas tanks big enough that no one needed to pit during green-flag racing. But eliminating the strategic opportunities behind pit-stop timing, and eliminating the pack's shuffling and reshuffling, would make the racing less exciting.

Eliminating pit-stop strategy would also make fewer racers and teams able to win races by deploying strategic rather than resource advantages. Bigger teams with more resources and better equipment might come to dominate the sport more than they already do. That outcome would not only eliminate excitement. It would also represent life and its possibilities less well.

The point of stock-car racing isn't simply to produce excitement. The deeper point of stock-car racing is to represent life and its possibilities well.

Pit stops represent life well. The human body and spirit doesn't simply run on forever. We all need and sometimes require breaks, for food, drink, sleep, medical care, family emergencies, or just to reset. The wise time those pit stops strategically.

Just watch a three-year-old boy, not yet having learned to pace himself and take breaks, tire himself out to the point of sobbing fits repeatedly. Or watch an arrogant professional, full of power and pride over professional influence and skills, ignore the natural rhythms a body and spirit need, until the professional crashes and burns in addictions, heart attacks, or strokes.

In pit stops and pit-stop strategy, stock-car racing has captured, represented, and symbolized a deep truth about life. Pressing ever forward without attention to its effects is counterproductive. One must nurture the body and spirit, and maintain healthy connections to communities, while pursuing one's own championship endeavors.

One doesn't win life's races and championships by sacrificing health, balance, and connections. Races and championships give their laurels to those who see, receive, and embrace all of life, not just the thin slices of life that a selfish hand may grab.

The shuffling and reshuffling of leaders also represent life and its possibilities well. We sometimes yearn for a relentless champion, whether in sports, politics, entertainment, business, or the professions. Wouldn't we finally see our rescue if a great one arose to solve all our problems? No, we would not. We would instead see tyranny, enslavement, and terrible loss. Good life, healthy life, life with balance, ambition, possibility, refreshment, and restoration, involves a shuffling and reshuffling of orders.

Every time pit-stop strategy reshuffles a stock-car race, race fans see new leaders with new stories, conflicts, skills, shortcomings, challenges, and opportunities. Each shuffling is like stepping away from an afternoon or evening of television, and a new show has come on. Each shuffling is also like waking up to a new season in one's own life.

Out on the track, with the race winding down, the three championship contenders ahead of Blake paused in battling one another for their false lead. Finally facing the realization that the whole racing world had by then reached, the three other championship contenders slowed around turns one and two and pulled off the track to make their last pit stop.

A flurry of other cars followed the leaders down pit road to make their own last pit stop. As they all sat trapped on pit road to take their four tires and gas, half the field flew by them out on the track, Blake among that half.

When the three other championship contenders came off pit road, Blake was well ahead of them, with a good number of other cars in between.

Insightful race fans and commentators knew that the gap that Blake now held over the other three championship contenders wasn't solely the result of pit strategy. Blake's lead over the other championship contenders was also the result of Blake's consistently better lap times, lap after lap.

Many would credit Blake's crew chief with the lead Blake now held over the other championship contenders, for the bold call the crew chief made to bring Blake's car in for a pit stop earlier in the race. The crew chief deserved credit for executing to perfection the strategy that he, Blake, and the race engineer developed.

But without Blake's finely tuned racing skills doing their work throughout the race, lap after lap, Blake would have had little gap ahead of the other three championship contenders. And those three contenders had fresh tires to close the gap.

The rest of the race wasn't without drama. The other contenders' fresh tires indeed meant that their lap times were better than Blake's lap times. The championship question, though, was *how much* better?

And that's where Blake's exquisite awareness of everything going on inside and outside his car kept making its difference. As the laps wound down toward the finish, the other contenders closed the gap but not as quickly as they needed to reach and pass Blake.

The late-race drama didn't just include Blake's diminishing lead over the other three championship contenders. The non-contending cars ahead of Blake were still driving for a race win.

Phoenix Speedway is an amazing track at which to watch a battle for the lead. Every part of the track's peculiar layout presents a different opportunity for passing.

The dive across the apron around turns three and four is the most dramatic of those opportunities. Fans hold their breath as the diving cars rejoin the cars that stayed on the racing surface around turns three and four, coming out of turn four. What advantage did the cars taking the shorter apron route gain over the leaders staying up on the racing surface? The corner wall at the end of turn four gives the dramatic answer.

Then, coming out of turn four, the leaders will often battle down the backstretch for the lead. A second-place car's dive low into turn one may force the leader up the track, or the second-place car's faster higher line around turns one and two may catapult the second-place car ahead of the leader coming out of turn two.

The frontstretch is the next passing opportunity, especially as cars prepare for their turn three entries. Which drivers will risk the greater corner entry speed? Too much speed sends the car up the track at turn three.

These were the battles that fans watched at the race's lead, while well back in the pack the three other championship contenders stalked Blake.

Battles throughout the racing field also risked a wreck and caution. A yellow caution flag would have bunched the field, cutting Blake's advantage over the three other championship contenders.

But no cars wrecked, no tires blew, and no engines failed as the laps counted down toward the finish.

Blake had his own challenges on track beyond trying to make every lap at the optimal speed. Blake was encountering and at times passing cars ahead of him. He couldn't simply run laps in place behind cars ahead of him. Blake needed to pass those cars, if he was going to make his best lap times to stay ahead of the other three championship contenders, who continued to gain on Blake on their fresher tires.

Blake, though, had an advantage in passing slower cars ahead of him late in the race. Championship-race etiquette sometimes dictates that non-contending cars give way to an obviously faster championship contender.

The same etiquette exists during any race, although not so powerfully as in the championship race. The custom, often altered to fit the circumstances, is that obviously slower cars should not hold up faster cars, especially when the slower cars have no chance of winning the race.

Blake thus didn't have to aggressively battle the slower cars he needed to pass. In most instances, the slower cars ahead of Blake pulled up the track or stayed low on the track, whichever Blake seemed most to need, so that Blake could pass without significant interruption of his speed.

Of course, the cars that the other three championship contenders were passing behind Blake did the same for them. But the three championship contenders were also racing one another. And those three did not give way to one another in the least, even when it seemed one of them was a bit slower than another.

With five laps to go, Blake was in seventh place. The nearest championship contender had closed to tenth place.

With three laps to go, Blake was in fifth place. The nearest championship contender had closed to seventh place.

With two laps to go, Blake was in fourth and the nearest championship contender in sixth.

And when the white flag flew, Blake was in third place with the nearest championship contender in fourth place, three car lengths behind Blake.

The entire crowd was of course on its feet for that last lap. They expected the championship contender to throw caution to the wind to reach and overtake Blake.

The crowd expected to see the championship contender behind Blake dive into turn one with such speed as to reach Blake and shove his car up the track.

But Blake's backstretch speed coming out of a perfectly timed turn four was so good that Blake slightly increased his lead to four car lengths. The championship contender was too far behind Blake to attempt that dramatic move.

Blake's braking into turn one was so perfectly timed, and his entry so perfectly aligned, that Blake held his lead through turns one and two. Blake maintained that lead down the frontstretch, leaving only turn three to navigate.

Blake had four car lengths of a lead to sacrifice on his turn three entry, to ensure that he did not overdrive the turn and lose the race at its last moment. Blake timed his braking and aligned his entry perfectly, sweeping around turn three as the championship contender behind him dove into turn three to make up the diminishing gap.

The two non-contending cars ahead of Blake flashed across the short chute's finish line under the checkered flag. Blake was next in third place. The championship contender behind Blake was at his rear bumper as they passed under the checkered flag.

Blake had finished third, but he had driven the perfect race. And he had won the Cup championship.

18

"Cup champion, Bud!" the crew chief radioed Blake after he crossed the finish line.

The crew chief expected to hear shouts from inside Blake's car. Instead, the crew chief heard nothing. The spotter Billy, though, was excited.

"You're the man!" Billy shouted over the radio.

Blake was silent inside the car for another moment before finally replying, "Thanks, guys. Great race."

Blake's voice sounded matter of fact, almost emotionless. Blake's car slowed on the track. Other cars began pulling up beside Blake's car for their drivers to give Blake a thumbs up in congratulations.

"How does it feel?" the crew chief said, bubbling with his own excitement.

"Feels great," Blake replied, again so matter of factly as to sound nearly emotionless.

Blake's car still crept along the track as Blake returned a thumbs up to the passing drivers. Up ahead, the driver who had won the race was doing a burnout in front of the grandstand.

"Thanks, Big Guy," the team owner's voice came over the radio, "Bring it home for the celebration."

"Glad to win another one for you," Blake replied, adding, "You're the best."

Blake pulled his car to a stop on the frontstretch, waiting for the race-winning driver to finish his burnout and on-track celebration.

That celebration would be brief and pro forma. Many would be glad for the race-winning driver, in this instance a rare winner who had driven an unusually strong race. But when a non-championship driver wins the championship race, that driver's duty is to briefly enjoy the race win before getting out of the way for the greater championship celebration.

Despite the sound of his voice over the radio, Blake hadn't felt emotionless or matter of fact in the immediate aftermath of his race win. Blake had instead not wanted his absorption in the race and moment to dissipate. He hadn't wanted the timeless spell of his perfect attunement with his surroundings to break.

Indeed, if Blake had a choice in the matter, he would have wanted the race to continue, even if it meant losing the championship.

In the latter half of the race, Blake had finally reached a pinnacle that he had long known existed but that he had not yet summited. Blake had not been trying to win a championship as much as he had been trying to reach that summit.

At the moment of his championship win, Blake could not have described that alternate summit, the true summit, satisfactorily. The championship itself would have to do as a stand-in for what Blake felt that he had actually finally received or accomplished. But it had something to do with having submitted utterly to the hierarchy in which he lived, so that the hierarchy's creator could attune him perfectly to it.

Blake knew that he had finally driven a race car as he had hoped to do throughout his life. And he further knew that his achievement had not been due to his greater or longer striving but due to his devoted preparation for receiving that gift.

As Blake watched the race-winning driver finish his burnout, the fine sense of attunement gradually dissipated. It had to do so. Blake would momentarily be doing his own burnout, when burnouts intentionally defame and destroy that fine attunement.

Blake regretted his attunement's dissipation, although he did not regret the burnout. Blake instead understood that the burnout was a proper tribute to the attuned state with his race car that he must lose to move into his next circumstantial awareness. He only hoped that he could indeed carry that attuned submission out of his race car and into the next stage of his life, especially with Diana.

Blake's burnout and on-track interview were over. Like pre-race festivities, post-race festivities have their own script. Blake was glad in the moment for the script because he would otherwise have been at a loss for words, his spirit still reaching for that pinnacle of attunement.

You see it in championship winners, race winners, and winners of other competitions and awards. You see that loss for words, when the public wants to hear what winning is like. Yet the public doesn't really want the words. We want instead to share in the attuned moment. We want the insight and inspiration, the restoration and transformation, that come with reaching the pinnacle where we meet the creator.

In his on-track interview, Blake thanked his crew chief, pit crew, and team owner. He thanked his manufacturer and sponsors. He thanked race fans. Blake also acknowledged the skill of the race winner and the other championship contenders, and the grace of the field in permitting the contenders to compete unimpeded.

But Blake did one other thing in his on-track interview, something that he looked forward to doing again, many more times and for a long time. He thanked Diana and told her he loved her.

Diana, Marla, and Rob were already descending from the celebrating corporate suites to the infield to greet and congratulate Blake, and join in the victory lane celebration.

The on-track interview concluded, and Blake climbed back in his car to roll back up the frontstretch and around onto pit road. Blake rolled the car slowly up pit road, accepting the congratulations of teams along the way, until he stopped the car in a swarm of well wishes at his pit stall.

Blake climbed from the car again to hug his crew chief, high five the race engineer, and hug and dance with his pit crew.

Diana, Marla, and Rob, among other well-wishers, hung respectfully back while Blake and the pit crew shared the joy and relief of the season-ending championship. It was over. They had won. They had no reason to do anything other than smile, laugh, dance, and celebrate.

Blake, though, soon shifted his gaze to search the celebration's perimeter for Diana. Blake's pit crew took his distraction as a signal to push his car toward victory lane in front of the huge grandstand, still filled with many fans.

Diana, Marla, and Rob caught Blake's gaze with waves. The four of them met in a big hug, until Marla and Rob pulled back to let Blake and Diana embrace and kiss. Those surrounding the happy couple cheered, as did fans still standing in the stands. None were anxious for the moment to end, even as the sun dipped toward dusk, and the great grandstand's shadows cloaked victory lane.

The Cup championship trophy's formal presentation followed in victory lane. Blake and his pit crew gathered in victory lane in front of the championship car for round after round of championship photographs. Diana took her turn next to Blake for several of those photographs, as did the team owner.

Marla and Diana together helped Blake navigate his evening's championship duties, including ensuring that Blake had sufficient food and fluid to manage.

Blake, for instance, had another on-track interview to complete after festivities died down, one prompting him to reflect at length back over the championship year. Blake and his interviewer each sat in director chairs on the track completing the long interview, as the sun disappeared. The track was by then mostly abandoned, but for pit crews still packing up and track crews clearing the grounds.

As Blake, Diana, and Marla prepared to leave the racetrack for the motorhome, after Blake's long interview, Blake stopped. A lone figure standing in the lower grandstands near the track had caught his eye.

Blake stared at the figure, while the figure stared back. Marla and Diana, standing beside Blake, followed his gaze until they, too, were looking at the figure.

Soon, the figure raised a right hand, giving a weak wave.

Blake paused before likewise raising a right hand for a weak wave back.

Marla uttered quietly out of one side of her mouth to Diana, saying, "It's our father."

After another moment passed, Blake looked at Marla, waiting for her response. Looking back at Blake, Marla tipped her head toward their father, indicating to Blake that he was free to go greet their father if he so desired.

Marla's slight motion also indicated to Blake that she was not accompanying him.

Blake next looked at Diana standing next to Marla. Blake waited for Diana's response.

Diana's mind told her to do exactly as Marla had done, tipping her head to give Blake her assent that he should go greet his father. But Diana's heart told her to join Blake in that greeting.

Diana took a deep breath, reached out her hand to Blake, and stepped forward to join him in walking over to greet their father.

But then, Diana hesitated. She looked up at Blake, catching his attention again, while she stopped and held his hand back so that he stopped, too.

Diana then turned back toward Marla, reaching out with her free hand for Marla to join them.

Tears were already streaming down Marla's face when Diana looked back toward her. But as Diana held her hand back toward Marla, inviting Marla to join them, Diana gave Marla the slightest nod, silently indicating that Diana would support her.

Marla nodded back, stepped forward, and took Diana's hand. The three of them, Blake, Diana, and Marla, walked over to greet the father at the edge of the track and grandstand.

The long separation of father from son and daughter had ended. None knew whether a relationship would or should follow.

Rob had other pressing responsibilities, after greeting, congratulating, and celebrating with Blake. Rob had his yurt friend up on Monument Hill, waiting for a ride home. Rob also had Blake's team owner to introduce to his yurt friend, as the team owner had requested.

When the team owner had finished with his victory lane photographs, he had stepped quietly aside from the celebration, as was his habit. Rob greeted him, whispering that their peculiar friend whom the team owner wished to meet was a short walk up Monument Hill. Rob could ask him to come down to meet the team owner.

The team owner shook his head, saying, "Let's go for a walk up Monument Hill. Good time to get out of here."

Rob led the way out the tunnel under the track and slowly up Monument Hill. He could see a lone party up the hill, toward which Rob and the team owner headed.

As they approached, Rob recognized not only his yurt friend but also the Munn family.

Rob was delighted to see that they had met. Rob hadn't planned their meeting, although he knew that both his friend and the Munn family were watching the race from Monument Hill. But then, Rob thought, that would be just like the peculiar former environmental activist Munn, to approach and make friends with an equally peculiar stranger.

Rob only thought of it later, as he related the event to Blake. But it also made symbolic sense that such disparate outsiders who had meant so much to Blake but who were foreigners to the stock-car community, would witness Blake's championship win together from the symbolic axis Monument Hill.

And it also made symbolic sense that Blake's team owner, who had meant even more to Blake, would climb Monument Hill to join them immediately after the championship win.

The symbolism of figures and events isn't merely about the meaning we impress on those figures and events. Symbolism isn't merely symbolic, Blake and Rob had come to understand. The yurt man himself had suggested that the mind doesn't impress meaning on symbols, which instead already hold the meaning that the mind only sometimes discerns and discovers.

Symbols are just another fractal level in the grand hierarchy, higher or lower than other similar meanings to which they point or that they reflect. The gathering of key figures up Monument Hill both gave Blake a pattern for his own minute behaviors while also reflecting the pattern of the divine constructs and entities at the mountain's top.

Blake and Rob had learned together, confirmed through the championship event, that the yurt man's insight isn't merely an intellectual achievement. Blake's interaction with the yurt man and exploration of his constructs had increased Blake's symbolic reasoning. It had shown Blake more of the divine architecture out of which flows the golden rule and every other rational pattern. It had invested every figure and every event with symbolic meaning, marrying the material with the divine.

"Greetings!" Rob called as he and the team owner reached the small party. He added, "Blake's team owner here wanted to meet you. I hope you enjoyed the championship race!"

The yurt man nodded solemnly, saying nothing.

Munn gave the team owner a kind handshake and congratulations before giving Rob a great hug. After smiling and greeting the team owner with polite congratulations, Munn's wife and two teens surrounded Rob, talking excitedly about the race.

The team owner stepped aside to where the yurt man stood, quietly looking into the distance. The team owner looked into the distance in the same manner. The two stood quietly, as if searching the fading horizon for some unrevealed but waiting meaning, while Rob and the Munn family continued their excited chatter behind them.

After a few minutes of silent staring, the team owner said simply, without averting his gaze from the horizon, "He's out there and up there, isn't he?"

The yurt man next to him nodded, also without breaking his gaze from the horizon.

After another minute passed, the team owner said, again without averting his gaze from the horizon, "He's drawn many things into alignment today, hasn't he?"

The yurt man next to him nodded again, again without breaking his gaze from the horizon.

After another minute passed, the team owner said, again while holding his gaze on the horizon, "I'm going to keep my eyes on him, hoping he shows me more."

Still without breaking his gaze from the horizon, the yurt man next to him said simply, "Me, too."

"Hey, well let's see," Rob was saying loudly to the Munn family behind the yurt man and team owner.

The team owner and yurt man turned back to the group.

"Munn and his family have offered our friend a ride back up his mountain," Rob shared, adding to his friend, "They'd love to see your yurt and lands. You've already heard this afternoon of their own enchanted lands, I understand."

"I'd enjoy that," the yurt man said with a small nod and smile.

The party began their descent from high on Monument Hill just at the precise moment that the sun dipped below the distant horizon.

Rob, the yurt man, and the team owner all noticed the perfect symbolism of even that last moment. Their eyes briefly met in small, secret smiles. They knew that their creator had enchanted the day from start to finish. He had pulled the cord taught to the last moment. And drivers, fans, friends, enemies, race cars, races, championships, and the hills and sun themselves had fallen perfectly in line in glorious worship.

19

"Cheers," Rob said, raising a glass in toast after everyone had settled around the residence's kitchen table.

Blake and Diana had met Rob and Marla at their residence Tuesday evening, just as they had throughout the regular season and championship playoffs. The season was over, but the season's rhythm had not yet subsided.

Because of Blake's championship win and Blake's extra duties the win engendered, they had all returned from Phoenix on Monday.

Blake had stopped by the race facility late in the day Monday, to greet and celebrate with the stay-at-home staff. They deserved a party with the champion, too. Blake had returned to the race facility early on Tuesday for season-end discussions, evaluations, and other duties.

The team's goal in the few days after the championship win was to plan the off season while freeing Blake and the rest of the team of major responsibilities for a rest and recuperation period, they hoped for the rest of the year. Team activities would accelerate again in January for the season's mid-February beginning.

Rob had spent late Monday and all day Tuesday on similar duties, discussing and evaluating security issues. The security team's goal was the same, to free the team's members of duties until early next year for a well-earned break.

Marla had public relations to which to attend for Blake, much more so than usual, given the welcome championship win. Marla's military PSYOPS background and type-A personality gave her one advantage in public-relations work that some other PR folks lack. Marla seldom let her guard down. She was always on duty.

That attribute served Blake well following the championship win. Winners often take a win as a reason to let go of customs and expectations. After all, shouldn't that be winning's reward, to relax? But winning creates its own expectations, elevated above the expectations following losses. And the winner who fails to meet those elevated expectations can quickly look like an unfit winner or even a loser.

Media appearances are just one of those extra obligations. Blake fulfilled another of those extra obligations of a winner when he gave special attention to the race facility's stay-at-home staff after his return from Phoenix. Those who aid in the win reasonably expect the winner's recognition.

Marla helped ensure that Blake also gave extra thanks and attention to his sponsors. Sponsors certainly gain with the win alone. Championship exposure can easily double or triple a sponsor's advertising value.

Blake had already done more for his sponsors by winning the championship than he could have done by just about anything else, including returning their every sponsorship dollar. But sponsor representatives still have feelings, not just advertising-value calculators. Marla helped Blake satisfy those feelings.

Diana helped Marla with her public-relations work, as part of Diana's continuing transition. Blake, Marla, and Diana had eased into a transition that every day seemed more clear, comfortable, and certain. Indeed, Marla was already beginning to quietly introduce Diana to sponsor representatives as Marla's replacement, although they hadn't yet planned a formal announcement of that transition.

Blake, Diana, Rob, and Marla made small talk around the kitchen table, as they enjoyed take-out food that Blake and Diana had brought with them to the residence. Rob and Marla hadn't yet found time to shop and cook since their return from Phoenix. They were all too exhausted, too.

The small talk was of fun and funny things that happened over the championship week and weekend. No one spoke of the championship itself. They instead spoke of the small personal things that close family members would share when gathering at home again after a work trip or vacation.

Marla shared a humorous interaction she had with a sponsor representative who had gotten so drunk in the corporate suite that he insisted that he would pay for another round of drinks, when the drinks were already free. The representative was a good friend whom Marla easily managed.

Diana shared a fun time that she had with the two other drivers' wives, away from the track on Friday. The wives had insisted on taking Diana on a shopping trip for things that they felt Diana might need for the wedding or afterward. In fact, though, they had just spent the time laughing, joking, and teasing, while they perused a popular shopping and eating district.

Blake mentioned a late-night outing on which the team's other three drivers had insisted Blake join them. He didn't disclose where they went or what they did, insisting that he left them to their own plans and devices at his earliest opportunity.

Rob shared the meeting of Blake's team owner with the yurt man and Munn family on Monument Hill.

The effect of the stories was just what the four of them needed to gather again in unity as a family.

It was also exactly what they needed for their conversation to turn to future plans for the family.

Rob had asked, foolishly as it turned out, whether the four of them should talk about the upcoming wedding, less than two months away.

"None of your business," Marla had chided Rob, teasing him and laughing as she did so.

"Diana?" Blake had asked, "Want to talk about plans?"

Diana shook her head, winking at Marla and then reaching over and giving Blake a pinch on the cheek.

"Well," Rob said with raised eyebrows exaggeratedly in a humorous fashion, "I guess we'll just leave it to you two, then."

They all laughed.

Instead, for the first time, the four of them discussed together the possibility of forming a race team.

Blake, they all knew, wasn't in any sense planning to leave his team owner. If sound precedent didn't already exist for other drivers having their own race teams, while continuing to drive for their team owner, Blake probably would never have considered it.

But that precedent had already demonstrated the benefits a driver and driver's family could draw from establishing and running their own racing organization, provided they did so in cooperation with the owner and team to whom the driver already had contractual and personal commitments.

Blake had already seen how his championship win had accelerated others' expectations for the next steps in his career. His championship interviewers had already asked about his next steps. Blake had deliberately declined to answer any of those questions, although he had ideas. Sharing those ideas, though, would only have fueled distracting public speculation.

Yet Blake was ready to hear from Diana, Marla, and Rob on what they thought they all might do next. Blake was especially keen on hearing what Rob and Marla thought might be their next venture.

Diana felt every bit as needful as Blake did to help Marla and Rob discern their next steps. Blake's career wasn't the question. Blake had a clear path forward, indeed, multiple potential paths. Blake would surely continue to race for championships. But he might also take on television commentary. He could start a podcast. He could expand his foundation work.

The paths and opportunities were not nearly so clear for Marla and Rob.

By evening's end, the four had discerned that a race team that Rob and Marla co-owned with Blake and Diana might be a good possibility. Marla would manage the team's operations. Blake would lead the team on the strategic and racing side. Rob's role and Diana's role they intentionally left undefined. Rob had more security work he wanted to do. Diana would already be taking on new roles with Blake, both marriage and public relations.

"Mind if Diana and I speak with Fred about it?" Blake asked Rob and Marla.

Rob and Marla looked at one another, shrugging. "Good idea," they said in unison, laughing for having done so.

Blake and Diana left together soon afterward. Blake dropped Diana off at her apartment, walking her to the door.

"Not many more nights of this, huh?" Blake asked as they stood outside Diana's apartment door.

Diana shook her head demurely as she looked up into Blake's eyes. They kissed and parted.

It took Blake and Diana a few days to arrange a meeting with Fred. Fred had asked about the meeting's purpose. They had indicated in confidence that it was to discuss a family racing team for a lower series. Fred had understood.

The three of them met at Blake's residence. Fred was the first to arrive. Blake met him at the door. Diana deliberately arrived thirty minutes late. She had wanted to give Blake and Fred an opportunity to speak privately.

When Diana arrived, Fred set to work asking them both questions from a list he had written out in pencil on a yellow pad. As was Fred's customary approach to such things, as an experienced psychologist and counselor, many of his questions evoked straightforward yes-or-no answers, each of which Fred recorded on his yellow pad.

Were they in any rush to do so? Fred asked, recording their *no* answer.

Have the four of them spoken with anyone else yet? Fred asked, again recording their *no* answer.

Would the team employ all four of them? Fred asked, recording their *probably not* answer.

Would they align the team with Blake's team owner? Fred asked, recording their *yes* answer.

Would they form the team if Blake's team owner preferred that they not? Fred asked, recording their *no* answer.

The inquiry proceeded in that fashion until Fred gradually began asking open-ended questions.

What was their goal? Fred asked, and *What would a good outcome look like?*

How might it affect their relationship with Rob and Marla? Fred asked, and *How might it affect their relationship with one another?*

Blake listened carefully to Diana and watched Diana closely, as Diana answered each question. Likewise, Diana listened carefully to Blake and watched Blake closely, as Blake answered each question.

Blake and Diana thus learned more about one another's insights, fears, hopes, and emotions than they learned anything from Fred. Indeed, Fred expressed no views or opinions. He mostly just asked questions.

When they were done, Fred went back over each of their answers, asking if he had recorded and summarized their answers correctly. The record that Fred made of those answers he might retain for a short time before disposing of it. The point wasn't that his record was correct or incorrect. The point was instead that by returning to each question and answer, Fred had given Blake and Diana an opportunity to hear and reconsider their answers.

Fred left with their profuse thanks. Blake and Diana remained, chatting about their impressions, further exploring their hopes and fears, and goals and dreams, for a possible race team. They agreed that they had many more conversations to share with Rob and Marla, and gradually with others. They also agreed that their timetable should be at least a year. And they soon shared their thoughts and impressions with a grateful Rob and Marla.

By the end of their first week back from the championship race, Diana and Marla were in top gear on their wedding planning and preparations.

They met on Friday over lunch, checklist in hand. Venue? Check. Dress? Check. Reception? Check. Band? In the works. Invitations? Check.

"Pastor?" Marla asked.

Diana gave Marla a blank look before saying, "Oh, that's right!"

They laughed. Diana had forgotten that a wedding requires a statutorily approved person to officiate, typically a pastor if not a judge or ship's captain.

Spending three out of four Sundays on the road interferes with church attendance and relationships. The traveling chapel services that Motor Racing Outreach offers at racing venues is a workable substitute, even for occasional weddings or memorials. But Blake and Diana still needed a pastor to officiate.

"How about Fred?" Marla asked.

"Fred?" Diana asked.

"He's a pastor," Marla replied.

Diana had forgotten or not known.

"I'll ask Blake," Diana replied.

"Good idea," Marla replied, causing both of them to laugh.

Down the checklist the two of them went, confirming what they had already accomplished and what remaining preparations they needed to do or assign.

"Honeymoon?" Marla asked with a sly smile at Diana.

"That one's on Blake," Diana replied with a similar smile, adding, "And he says he's got the perfect plan."

Marla raised her eyebrows, saying, "And you trust him?"

They both laughed.

Soon, they completed their list. Marla, though, raised another issue about which Diana hadn't thought.

"Anyone giving away the bride?" Marla asked.

Diana frowned before asking, "Do we have to do that?"

"No," Marla replied, "You can walk down the aisle alone."

They looked at one another in seriousness. Then they both smiled and laughed.

Diana's own father had left when she was still young and had disappeared and apparently passed away long ago, according to the last account of Diana's mother.

"You know," Diana said after a little more thought, "I think I'd prefer to have an appropriate escort."

"Well then, Missy," Marla teased with a smile, "Whom do you have in mind?"

Diana thought in silence. Marla thought of joking again but instead respectfully gave Diana the time.

"I do know of a possibility," Diana finally said.

"Care to share?" Marla asked.

"You may not like it," Diana replied.

Marla looked back at Diana, squinting and giving Diana a tilt of her head, having no idea yet of whom Diana might propose. But then, Marla realized whom Diana meant. Marla pressed her lips together and closed her eyes in thought as Diana watched. Finally, Marla opened her eyes to look at Diana.

"Better ask Blake," Marla said.

"I will," Diana replied, nodding. Diana reached across the table to gently place her hand on Marla's forearm.

"You'll tell me if not, right?" Diana asked.

Marla nodded.

20

"Well," Marla whispered to Rob as they stood at the front of the Speedway Club, looking to the back of the Club where Diana was about to enter in her wedding dress, "I think everyone they invited is here."

Indeed, three-hundred handsomely outfitted men and elegantly dressed women filled the Speedway Club. They smiled and waved discreetly at one another as they awaited Diana's entry.

Rob leaned over to whisper back to Marla, "Wait until you see the Fillmore later tonight for the reception. It'll be packed."

Blake stood in front of Rob and Marla, also facing the back of the Club, where Diana was about to enter. Blake looked composed, poised, and regal. He also looked eager and joyful.

Stealing glances at her brother in front of her, while keeping an eye out for Diana's impending entry to the rear, Marla loved, admired, and respected Blake more than ever.

Marla was also happier for Blake than ever. Marla had once thought that nothing could make her brother happier than winning a Cup championship. She knew now that she had been quite wrong. Winning Diana was making Blake far happier than any championship.

Fred stood behind Blake, ready to preside. While waiting for Diana's entry, Fred took a moment to search out his own wife among the guests. Seeing her, he winked and smiled. She smiled back while slightly raising a scolding finger in jest. It was not the time for anything other than perfect decorum, as both knew.

Less than two months had passed since Blake's championship win. The time had passed quickly, filled with the joy of the Thanksgiving and Christmas holidays and the greater joy of wedding anticipation.

The wedding invitations had brought Blake and Diana first a trickle and then a flood of happy communications.

Some replies were simple confirmations of attendance, with appropriate congratulations. Other replies, though, included brief or lengthy accounts of memories shared with one or the other of the wedding party.

Blake and Diana read the replies together, filling one another in on the background for the accounts, some of them surely embellished. With each confirmation, Blake and Diana learned more of one another's friends and experiences.

Many happily married couples can confirm that learning at least some of their spouse's history can promote understanding and trust within the marriage relationship. The accounts that guests shared in their replies, on which Blake expanded, gave Diana a fuller picture of the man whom she was about to marry, without diminishing her view of him in the least. The same was true for Blake, as he learned more about Diana. They might have lived as husband and wife for years without having discovered the things that the guests' replies revealed or triggered.

Blake's team owner was of course among the guests. Diana could have asked the owner to walk her down the aisle, given the highest regard in which Diana and Blake both held him. Diana had not. She had heard a slightly higher call.

Billy the spotter and his wife were also among the guests. A driver never forgets his spotter, although Blake had a suspicion that Billy would later join the band if they let him, or usurp the stage if the band didn't invite him, to stir the reception to its greatest fun.

The centenarian Lightnin' was not among the guests, although Blake and Diana had certainly invited her. Lightnin' had been nearly the only invitee to decline, saying that her habit on New Year's Eve was to turn in early and that she didn't want to leave in the middle of the reception and spoil the wedding party's fun.

Guests stirred at the back of the Speedway Club, where Diana was about to make her entry.

And then, Diana appeared at the Speedway Club's entry way. She looked stunning.

Anyone present would, if placed under oath, have said that at that moment, Diana was by far the most beautiful woman in the room, as is fitting and true at every wedding. If any man had said otherwise at that moment, even to their own gorgeous wife, they would have lied. They could speak truly later to their own wife that their own wife was far more beautiful. But at the moment of her entry for the nuptials, the bride is always the most beautiful in the room.

Diana, though, was not walking alone. She instead entered on the arm of a figure whom only Blake and Marla any longer recognized. Their father would give away the bride.

* * *

Far above the happy nuptials, the divine council convened.

Seraphim surrounded the throne. Their fiery light drove away to the farthest reaches of heaven anything but the greatest brilliance to emanate from the throne. Two of their six mighty wings covered their faces so that the creator's presence wouldn't shatter them. Two more of their wings covered their feet so that their proximity would not offend the throne. And their last two wings stood ready to raise them in furious flight at the creator's least command.

The seraphim briefly made way, as the creator, a slight figure just like that of a man but with pierced side, hands, and feet, descended toward his throne. As soon as the creator reached and sat on his throne, the seraphim once again surrounded him. Simultaneously, the many millions of divine entities present, so many and so pure as to look like a sea of glass stretching without end before the throne, fell to their faces in utter adoration of their creator. Glorious song echoed up and back off heaven's distant ceiling, through which the creator had descended.

The creator took a deep breath and exhaled, gently and naturally, almost as if in a sigh after waking from a pleasant afternoon nap. Yet his effortless breath spread forth across the millions of divine entities like a great wave, carrying with it the deepest and most profound meaning, inspiration, rationality, and intention. The millions of divine entities gratefully received and incorporated the creator's breath as the magnificent power and love and light that it in fact was, readying them once again to carry that breath to the ends of creation for the good that the creator desired.

But then, a roar of wonder went up from the millions of divine entities before the great throne. A figure from the earth far below had appeared, crouching and holding tightly to the back of a fearsome seraphim winging straight for the throne. As the seraphim approached the throne, it slowed and descended until it had alighted before the throne. It shook the figure rudely off its back, tumbling the figure to the brilliant glass floor at the throne's foot.

The seraphim surrounding the throne parted, so that the poor figure lying prone on the glass floor could look up toward the throne. The creator, no bigger but significantly slighter than the figure whom the seraphim had dumped, looked down toward his friend. The creator tipped his head toward the nearest divine entity, indicating that the entity should help his poor friend to his feet. With the divine entity's assistance, the figure stood, brushed off his mountaineering clothes, and straightened his large bushy beard. The figure blinked, straight faced and serious, at the creator, tipping his head slightly this way and that way to be sure he was seeing with appropriate clarity.

And then the creator spoke. As he did so, the sea of divine entities before him rolled with the thunder of the creator's voice, exulted at the majesty of the creator's inspiration, and quaked with holy fear over the command of the creator's intention. The chunky, bearded figure in mountaineering clothes standing before the creator, though, simply blinked again, this time turning one ear toward the creator to be sure that he had heard the creator's voice rather than the wind in the branches or the gurgling of the brook.

The creator first expressed to his friend the creator's gratitude for heeding the creator's desire that his friend go meet and speak with the racer, and to have shared the creator's words with the racer in messages. The creator next expressed to his friend that the creator would have other desires for his friend to carry out, especially, though, that his friend continue to look to the creator's mountaintop. The creator then called for the mighty seraphim who had dumped the poor figure before the creator to return his bearded friend to the earth.

The poor figure once again mounted the seraphim's back, quaking in fear as he did so. The seraphim rose into the air with a great flap of its mighty wings and, with another flap, shot off across the sea of divine entities below them. The bearded man clung to the seraphim's back. But the bearded man summoned the courage to look back toward the creator, just as the seraphim turned in the air to dive down through the sea of divine entities back to the earth. And as the bearded man did so, he saw and heard the creator issue another command, carried by the creator's breath across the sea of divine entities.

**

The yurt man awoke with a start. Had he just dreamed of the creator at the mountaintop? After all these years of living alone in contemplation of the divine, had he just heard the creator's own voice? Or had it been the sound of the wind in the trees and the gurgling brook? The yurt man tossed and turned in his yurt bed, unable either to grasp or to shake what he had just experienced or dreamed. But just as he prepared to drift asleep again, the yurt man remembered that it was New Year's Eve. And he remembered, too, that Blake and Diana had planned to wed that night.

And then, an impression began to form in the yurt man's mind. The impression was that he had just heard the creator's voice command his divine entities that the racer and his bride whose nuptials were taking place that night would be his forever, that no harm would ever touch them, that they would live a long and happy life on earth in which they brought forth many happy and healthy children and enjoyed many happy and healthy grandchildren, and that when their earthly life ended they would join him in heaven as his, to live forever in his glorious embrace. And in response, a great cry of joy rang out across heaven, saying *Let it be done.*